GW00457613

**Derbyshire boy
rural middle England as it was**

John G Smith

John G Smith

Dedication

This book is dedicated to the
memory of my mum and dad

I have to thank all those that gave me a start in life

Disclaimer

All persons and organisations mentioned in this book are
real. If I have caused offence to any party, this was
unintentional and not wilful. All events described in this
work reflect my honest recollection and interpretation

Derbyshire boy

Red Barn Farm – today

- and circa 1850

John G Smith

The author aged six.....

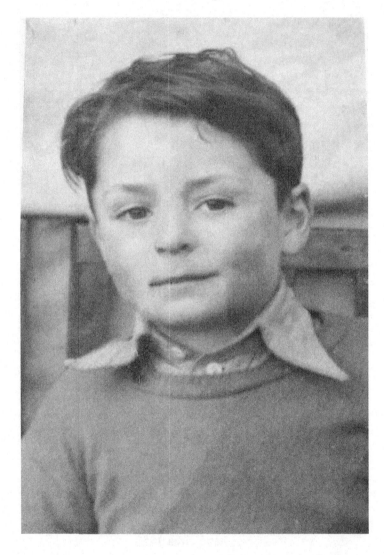

Chapter one
Rough hewn

The demarcation between bottom-enders and top-enders was very marked and well understood in the late 1940s. The war had made little difference. This was not a proper village. Rather, it was a community thrown together, first by the coal-mines, later the railways. The housing was cheap. In the bottom-end, the terraced houses were even cheaper and more closely packed than in the top-end. The dividing line was the war memorial and the church hall. The latter was something of a travesty since there was actually no church. The church was a mile away down Cragg Lane to Old Blackwell, a tiny but genuine old village with small stone cottages and whose only concession to the current times was a red-brick Victorian pub.

The Robin Hood (or "Thack" as it was known) had been built to serve the Irish navvies who cut the deep channels needed to take the Great Central Railway line en-route to Edinburgh and, most importantly in its day, its crack train the Master Cutler. The southern link from Annesley in Nottinghamshire had been opened for coal freight in July 1898 and the following March the first passenger train delivered its customers in some comfort to London Marylebone under the slogan *Rapid Travel In Luxury*. It was no gimmick. A fourth main route to the capital had arrived.

Rather ironic that we are in Newton as derived from the old English for "new farm" and yet, with your patience, I will take you to an old farm and describe its ways and its people. Newton had little going for it except its location. It lay on the border of Sherwood Forest, as determined by surveys in the fourteenth and sixteenth centuries, when it was a royal forest.

What Newton did have was a methodist chapel. This was planted decisively in the bottom-end and was looked down upon in a most un-Christian way by those in authority in the church and, most particularly, by those who ran the church hall. This might have been not so much generic as specific to my Great Aunt Pem (her proper name was Emily although I never heard anyone call her that). She was a most formidable woman. A spinster school teacher all her working life and now well into retirement, she exerted authority over the young, poor and innocent Sunday school attendees. These, despite a good deal of pressure and cajoling did not include me.

Other than day school, which to me was barely acceptable as compulsory, my abject refusal to join any group activity extended to the youth club, boy scouts, boys brigade and most probably others. I wandered the pit-hills as a loner, picked wild flowers for mum as a loner, started to help dad with the cows as a loner and as a loner I would stay. Being sure that those attending Sunday school were learning good things (such children included my sister) was soon tempered by a growing belief that in equal measure they were poisoned against chapel. According to Great Aunt Pem, nothing good ever came of going to chapel. Yet, some of the friends made at day school went to chapel instead of Sunday school and actually liked it. Most of the songs were jolly and the games loads of fun. It was hard to see what was wrong with chapel or why those attending were absolutely banned from riding on the carts, lorries and other assorted floats which made up the Whitsuntide procession.

The methodist chapel was hardly an upstart although it could not compete with the history of St Werburgh's church in Old Blackwell to which my Great Aunt Pem's Sunday school was affiliated. The chapel was opened in 1904 and was paid for by the local people and this no doubt was the genesis of its popularity. The feud betwixt church and chapel goes back much further. Prior to about 1860, the vicar of Blackwell Church held services in a farm building, but then a disagreement arose and the building was taken over by the Primitive Methodist Church, Mansfield Circuit. A split. It is interesting to dwell on how the orderly if disharmonious village society of the 1940's had evolved. This older chapel had a table with inkwells so that the children could learn to write and so education via religious instruction had arrived.

Disaster struck in 1877, the roof of the chapel collapsed. The only available space was the *club* room in the New Inn public house. The problems arose at holiday times as this special room was used for county festivities uppermost of which were competitions between local bands. When the club room could not be used as a chapel the room over the blacksmith's shop or the goods room of the Midland Railway Station (down the bottom end of the village heading towards Tibshelf) was used. It is so easy now to take for granted the status quo. Back then, village people had to make do with whatever there was. And things did change very slowly, at any rate by today's standards. Well into the 1960's my dad still went to the New Inn on a Friday night to "pay my club" (meaning a subscription to the charity Druids that could be fallen back on in times of sickness and indeed death) and my cousin Edwin still rehearsed his cornet and piano accordion for the local band.

It became accepted that I had regular jobs to do for Great Aunt Pem. These included filling up the coal bucket from the coal-house, sweeping up the paths and driveway and posting letters. This latter activity never failed to fill me with amazement because at the instant of being asked, the letter or letters had not even been written. There I stood, mesmerised by the rapid scribbling which no doubt told the distant cousin in the Isle of Wight that a young nervous great-nephew was still performing the chores. A further regular job introduced a few years later was to fetch five-shillings-worth of best steak from Browns the Butchers down the road. The best thing about this chore was that I was paid. Great Aunt Pem was my sole source of pocket-money.

In the earliest days uncle Jack, an elder brother of Great Aunt Pem, lived with her. He was a cripple. Both of his legs were withered and he could only move with the aid of crutches. It was rumoured that he had been dropped by an aunt soon after birth. The full story never quite emerged and the aunt in question was never revealed. He was a very kind man and kept biscuits in a red tin in the cupboard to his left-hand side. I never called without him giving me a biscuit. Much later, I was told by a venerable old lady who was always referred to with great respect as Mrs Housley, and who owned one of the few original cottages in Newton, that as a young man uncle Jack had gone drinking with his pals "just as if he was normal". She added that he could propel himself from pub to pub as fast as any of them and that if a fight broke out he could brandish his crutches to great effect. I never knew if this was true but I was very sad when he died. I missed the questions he always bombarded me with when trying to catch me out on the farm gossip. I missed the red tin and its contents too.

Many years later I would sit with Great Aunt Pem on Saturday evenings and play the card game *canasta* and sometimes on Sunday afternoons listen to *Flotsam and Jetsam* and George Cole on the radio. By then she was mellowing and I was more confident. She outlived her nephew Edmund who looked after her in later years. She lived to be 94.

A proper village would have been in a proper county. Even that didn't apply. Although strictly in Derbyshire, Newton was not a Derbyshire village. Derbyshire villages are pretty, always on steep hillsides so that walkers can "do the Peak District" and the houses are made of stone. In fact it was right on the Nottinghamshire border. The brook which forms the border is also the parish as well as the county boundary.

The source of this brook was an area we knew as Whiteborough. It was high ground to the east and close to Tyburn's Hill where highwaymen had been hung. Crossing the road near the Woodend Public House (Sherwood Forest was the wood in question), it ran along the hedge bottom of my dad's field to join another brook that had come from over *dimmy* – originally Demonsdale. I will tell the sad tale of this second brook a little later as this story unfolds.

Mrs Housley could remember as a little girl walking for miles from Newton eastwards without seeing a single household or meeting a soul. Without knowing it, she would have been on the Peveril Way skirting the edge of Sherwood Forest. This route was used in the days of William the Conqueror to travel between Alfreton and Bolsover. It was named after William Peveril who controlled much of northern England and resided in both Bolsover Castle and Peveril Castle in Castleton. Alfreton was the seat of the Lord of Alfreton who was also the Sheriff of Nottingham. This squares the historical circle. The Manor of Blackwell was part of the domain of the Lord of Alfreton. Nondescript Newton was in the parish of Blackwell.

In such a backwater setting, the differences between bottom-enders and top-enders could never be cosmetic. The rough, and it had to be said for particular families dirty, bottom-enders were actually at war with the more refined top-enders. This was from time to time a real war fought out in pitched battles on Tommy Newnies rough ground just this side of the woodyard that formed a natural barrier with the residents of the next village of Tibshelf. These were scary do's that I was careful to avoid and the scars of battle, as appearing on the kids in the schoolyard, always seemed justification enough. At the far side of Tommy Newnies was the railway line that higher up the steep incline would traverse my dad's top field. On the other side of the railway line was the site of the Tibshelf Bottom Pit with its still open brick kilns, the product of which built most of the houses in Newton. The mist

of time is clearing like the mist that had hung low over the bottom field. It was early spring and, as I had hoped, the violets were spread out beneath the hedge almost hidden by a mass of broad thick leaves and in tight clumps on the ditch side. For some unknown reason it was the only place on the farm they could be found and so very tiny. You had to know exactly where to look.

Looking back now I suppose they should not have been picked. Left as one of nature's treasures from probably centuries past. A place left as rough pasture, not even worth fertilizing for early eating grass since this fringe of the pit-hills was unworkable. So were the pit-hills themselves, or so I was later to be told and would come to appreciate. Of course not now. This was the most magical adventure land. That little bunch of violets were in a small hand and taken with much pride back to the bottom gate over the stile (which was never crossed without an expectant look at the small indentation on the huge stone foot-slab that had once, and only once, held a cuckoo's egg) to start the long steep climb through the little field. Then past the gate to the rough pieces field that lay parallel to the fresh-water spring and on up the field below the stack yard to approach the top knob until the first chimney pot of the farmhouse came into view.

Now came the measure of the climb and the gradual reward for the effort as successively more of the chimneys came into view. Now the red tip of the roof, now the blue, now the gable-end of the eastern eaves and finally the pigsty's galvanised roof as simultaneously the farmyard gate and stackyard were on the last one hundred yards or so of level if undulating grass field.

That hard little journey would be taken so many times as to be so etched into a small mind to be as clear now some sixty years later as it was wearisome then. Slogged in winter in mud churned by tractor and trailer tyres; in summer hindered by deep hard ruts baked from the same rough transport and in the seasons between sloshed in Wellington boots wet from heavy dew or drizzle or downpour. Once, it was done in fog so thick that the certain straight line from the rough pieces gate to the top knob went bewilderingly wrong. A first push into unknown territory with no familiar pointers. Disorientation, disbelief at setting out when a path with clear markers was so much a better bet. Deep self-doubt was quickly all enveloping. Did the fact that eventually a hedge was reached, that an enforced decision of left or right had to be taken, influence the future?

There were more than violets of course. It's just that they always seemed to be the genesis. My mum teaching "there is a flower that shall be mine, it is the little celandine". We never knew the proper names. Cowslip, may-blob, ladysmock, egg and bacon plant, peckeye, scarlet pimpernel, red campion. It was so natural to know them, pick them and bring them back to the kitchen, as in the early Spring the catkins and pussy-willows.

The countryside today is empty, handed over to crops and machinery. But it was not always so. People walked to work, walked to take the air, walked to play in the fields with children, walked for pleasure. The three old men fascinated me. Each one must have been at least 150 years old. So bowed were their backs, so slow their pace. And why was one always behind the other two? Where had they started out from and where were they going to? Always the same route, down from Huthwaite and up our land towards Newton. And the vicar of Huthwaite church, always walking alone and always with a stick that he used to poke into the hedge bottom and out of sight, any bit of paper that was lying around. Was he just a bit eccentric? Was he composing his next sermon? Was he a bit mad? And the midgets. There was Little Nell and her husband Little Bill. They also walked through and were always

laughing and joking. Have all the small people died out or just,
like everyone else, merely stopped walking the fields?

In the earliest days, before the grey Ferguson 35 tractor
appeared, there were two working horses. One was called
Violet and the other was Daisy. Small delicate names for big
awkward things. Always the most awkward when made to
back into the shafts, that is, pulled backwards onto the bridle
and bit and into the cart. Two very different carts stick in my
mind. One synonymous with lightness and one with heavy
work. In the first category (or so it seems to me now) was the
summer Sunday "after tea" (and very rare) trip out in the horse
and *tub*. This two-large-wheeled cart with its hinged back door
would be taken up Woodlane, over Wildhill to Teversal,
touching Pleasley and back via the tight narrow lanes leading
to and from Hardwick Hall. The other use was daily. It was
really work but did not seem to be. Two churns of milk, ten to
twelve gallons on a good day, had to be taken each morning to
the wooden stand at the end of Goodalls' Drive in the village
in time to catch the Co-op lorry. This brought in my dad's sole
regular income of any note from Red Barn Farm. The second
cart was a truly multi-purpose monster. It carried muck for
spreading, brought in hay and corn-sheaves (wheat and oats),
humped turnips, mangolds and kale and carried all the tools for
fencing and ditching.

In those early days, Violet and Daisy were first and
foremost not recognised for their use but simply as huge,
warm, hairy and plodding friends. Hairy because of the
flowing mane that had to be hung onto for grim death once I
was lifted aloft onto that enormous high back. Hairy too,
because of my slipping in the mud and then being galloped
over without a scratch.

So, here we are in this magical wonderland. Wild flowers,
trees, hedgerows, up-hill walks home, horses, milking the
cows and spreading the muck, and bringing in the crops and
the first Fergie 35 and no thought of incarceration at school.
But it had to come and it did come as certain as a fifth birthday
with angel cake and jelly.

A reluctant drag across the back field, over the stile and up
the lane to cobbler's path leading directly to the school playing

field and two wooden huts known as Infants but which were actually open prisons that were not open. Hatred wasn't in it. Of the abrupt end to freedom, of the mindless paper exercises, of the noisy others in the way, of the place itself but most of all of the adults in it and of the very institutional effrontery. This wanton disregard for what I wanted and needed was never to go away. Here's John Smith from the Red Barn. He'll help you read, and now that you are behind, he'll help you catch up and (somewhat later) "I'll do your sums but you have to be in my gang".

I do have this big advantage. A paradise to play in after school and Saturdays. It sets me apart. There is one other big asset. It seems that I can sing. In a few years this will send me to the important Southwell Minster *out of the rut* school to be tested. But I did not know my music theory despite the best after-hours tuition from Miss Pollard and so failed the entrance exam. My dad took me by bus on the long journey to Southwell for the examination. So why if he was so keen to see me get on at this early age was he so equally keen to hold me back later?

A motley collection may seem a hackneyed expression for those friends that were regular visitors to the farm and who were on my side. Nevertheless, it is apt. For a start there was Terry Haydon. He must have come from a strange family albeit, as far as I ever knew, a stable one. I never once got invited to his home, which was unique amongst my friends, and he had a propensity to brag in an extraordinarily exaggerated way about the feats of his dad. He told my mum whilst eating biscuits in the kitchen that his dad had jumped clean over a double-decker bus. This was acquiesced with great seriousness. The reason for his clear favouritism with my mum was his ability, willingly demonstrated on any occasion, to play the mouth-organ. I think he must have had a lot of natural raw talent because years later as a teenager he led a group of local lads, complete with a manager who, as the Newtones, actually made a record (or so rumour had it). Whither a pre-Beatles Lennon or a pre-skiffle Lonnie? His other two attributes were first that whilst the rest of us home-made our adventure toys, Terry could always produce a super shop-bought job courtesy of his fabulous dad. A fantastic bow and arrow set and later a box-kite certainly fell into this category. Secondly, and at an incredibly early age, he was the first to smoke. Eventually, he was to get me started although I had reached the middle teen years (just).

Then there was Dougie Berresford and he was reckoned to be just slightly better than the rest of us partly because his home was as near to a proper cottage as existed in the village and just past the war memorial but mainly because his parents were both school teachers. The location of the Berresfords' cottage placed it neither in the top end or the bottom end of Newton. Rather, it was in the centre and amongst a number of business premises that were quite different to the houses that people actually lived in.

A large proud Victorian building housed on its upper floor a billiard hall as testament to the then craze with the celebrity Joe Davis ruling the roost. Very apt since Joe had been born in the Derbyshire mining village of Whitwell which was not far away. On the ground floor of the building was a general store leading from the petrol station. More important than petrol as a fuel was the sale of paraffin, since it was a household as well as an agricultural necessity. Our lamps at home were all paraffin fuelled and started by methylated spirits, a fuel in its coloured form also stocked by Shane Butler's dad who owned the store. This store had two other great attractions. It sold giant tubs of ice cream, the cardboard lid of which was used to scoop out the delicious contents. The second rather unusual and desirable offering was quart (not pint) bottles of dandelion and burdock pop.

Across the road from the billiard hall was the cobbler's shop. This was a fabulous world to enter. The smell of newly worked leather and the array of interesting tools became an allure far beyond the occasional need to visit. And this need may be more basic than just taking in shoes or boots. It might be to buy actual leather since my dad, like many others, had his own hobbing foot with its different sizes of metal feet. The boot to be repaired would be shaped around the metal foot using the new piece of leather and a sharp knife, before being nailed into place with special tacks and a heavy hammer. So the cobbler had a vertically integrated business and this was the secret of his survival over so many years in the smallest of villages. Mend, yes, but also sell the raw materials and, moving up the chain, he could sell you new working boots, heavy shoes and the ever-essential Wellington boots. He might even leather patch certain garments. A wonderful man was the cobbler.

Further down the street was a newsagent/general grocer and further down still, a take-away chip shop. This most popular establishment was *the* stopping off place when the New Inn closed its doors late at night and, for a different section of village life, at Saturday midday. So staple were fish and chips that the village boasted a second shop although this was positioned four-square in the top end and consequently was somewhat more salubrious.

For those wanting more variation in the otherwise cod or haddock fish diet, there was the weekly visit of the mussel man who walked the streets with a large basket on his shoulders and sold by the pound weight to anyone stopping him or, as a last resort, the shrimp man might appear late in the evening in the New Inn or The George & Dragon or the working men's club. Otherwise, and short of a trip to Chesterfield some ten miles away, wet fish was unavailable. Perhaps that is why a tin of red salmon from the co-op was such a rare luxury. Of course the high price of a tin played its part too.

The old houses where Dougie lived were in a tight group whose names, like the properties themselves, have long since been consigned to history. Shooters Row, Shooters Yard, Nan's Nick and best of all Morning Star Terrace. Shooter was a family name and Moe Shooter had a smallholding on land behind these houses. It was a wonderful place to visit as a small boy and visit we did because my dad often grazed his cows on Moe's field. To do so, the cows had to be driven through the heart of the village and even in those quiet times this journey had its own peculiar excitement, not least when a beast might decide to empty its bladder or bowels in front of someone's front gate or worst still, in the middle of the road. My dad carried a bucket and brush especially for the purpose of reparation but this could be too rushed to be wholly effective if, at the same time, a second animal decided to take a route other than the one to Moe's place and I had raced off to get it back on track.

As he had such a small place, Moe turned his hand to growing things for the local market in his many and magnificently heated greenhouses. His speciality was tomatoes and there must have been some sort of trade-off between our cows keeping his grass under control and fertilized and his supply of all the tomatoes my mum could possibly use. I always picked the tomatoes since my dad was too engrossed in talking to Moe whilst both leaned on the fence. They always had much to discuss.

Not that I cared about any delay in getting back home due to Moe's other speciality feature, the pond. We didn't have a pond except the one near the pit hills and there was not much in that apart from the usual frog spawn and toad spawn. But Moe's had loads of interesting creatures all through the year and the spawn actually developed into tadpoles and then tiny frogs and then bigger frogs and they were everywhere. And then, just as we found them in the bigger ponds down George Hollins's lane, there were the newts. To me, they were little dragons and as with George and the big dragon, had to be mastered. So, I took a few back home and put them in the big horse trough outside the cowhouse door. Try as they might, the little amphibians could climb only about half way up the steep sides of the trough before falling back down. The frequent lack of any water in the trough, due to the thirst of the cows let in from the field, added to the misery of the newts and exaggerated my cruel action of imprisoning them. Whether in that hell hole or in Moe's paradisiacal pond, their differing sizes and colouration was the subject of great boyhood wonder along with the alligator walk and trailing long tail. My favourites were the large spotted-back specimens. I was fascinated too by the water boatmen and as the summer drew on the blue, green and purple dragonflies. My first point of call at Moe's place was always the pond, I can see it and smell it now.

Somehow, having our farm and visiting Moe's place draws a parallel with the Sunday evening costume dramas that the

BBC seem able to regurgitate with regular ease. Not the costume or necessarily the drama but the distinction between the haves and the have nots. My dad and Moe both had land and a bit of a business. They were not wealthy or privileged but they were set apart. For example, on that short journey between the two places, we would pass a terraced house occupied by a large family. This family was regarded as not too clean and there were many, many children. These children had afflictions. Too many fingers on one hand, strange appendages on a face. My skin used to crawl every time we passed their front door. How would these have nots climb out of this horse trough?

Dougie was generally recognised as being pushed. Not surprisingly he was the only one in our year to pass the 11 plus examination. This bestowed elitist status since the grammar school was some miles away and demanded a special bus and he got robed in a special uniform. Inevitably he would leave our humble circle. Not that that mattered when we were fighting on the hay-stacks, having pitched battles in the back field with vicious home-made wooden swords and guarded with dustbin lid shields or playing hide and seek on the pit-hills. Indeed, Dougie was if anything disadvantaged since uniquely amongst an exceedingly skinny lot, he was a bit on the chubby side.

Brian Sheriff was somewhat from the wrong side of the track. A miner's son, he lived in the bottom end and the only one of my friends to do so apart from Ossie Rhodes. Brian was always very cheerful, good looking in a happy sort of way and had flaming red hair. He was destined to follow the family pattern and start his working life in the coal-mine although as an apprentice electrician which, whilst paying much less, was recognised as a considerable step up from working on the coal-face.

One surprising turn of events was that the Sheriff family was the first in the village to acquire a television set. Perhaps it should not have been surprising since coal-face miners such as his dad earned top wages and their home was most likely rented and not owned, but even so, a television was very expensive and regarded as a new-fangled luxury. *Acquire* in this sense means shop bought. It was not the first TV in the village to be viewed. My uncle Jack (married to aunt Madge) had that. He made it himself. He worked for an electronics manufacturer in Mansfield called Whiteleys. The set he brought home had a nine-inch screen and a minor defect. The defect, that was more pronounced on the set he made later for uncle Ernie, caused the picture to roll sporadically. But, being a clever electrical engineer, uncle Jack provided a solution. There was a small hole near the bottom of the case that held the tiny screen. Into this hole had to be inserted a knitting needle. Sometimes it worked and the rolling stopped, sometimes it did not. Uncle Ernie, being an ex-war veteran, had a sort of way with bad words.

I was very lucky to be Brian's friend and to be invited to watch a sort of detective series in which the hero had this habit of throwing a jelly bean in the air and catching it in his open mouth. It showed his skill and dexterity, things I did not possess having tried it with my, rarely able to afford, chocolate raisins sold in a wonderfully coloured rectangular shaped cardboard box. I wondered if jelly beans were smaller than chocolate raisins.

Brian was especially keen for me and a few other boys to see, when his mum and dad were out, the Tiller Girls perform on the Black and White Minstrel show. We watched those long slim legs kick into the air and we could see just about everything. Brian was a real mate. Sometime later he was also a real mate to his dad, pushing him in a wheelchair to the George & Dragon on a Sunday lunchtime for his pint. As was common, the coalface over too many years had taken its toll. Tragically, Brian himself was destined to die young.

My closest friend in those infant and junior school days was Kenny Milward. He was a top ender and lived with a very respectable mum and dad in Sherwood Street in a linked terraced house next to a gimmal (alleyway). I do not recall ever falling out with Kenny and we became pretty much inseparable. Interestingly and like Terry, he did not find work as would be preordained in either a manual or technical job but in retail. Terry went into a sports shop in Nottingham and Kenny an electrical goods and radio shop in Huthwaite.

Perhaps retail or at any rate service was at home in this street of terraced houses. A Mr Wiltshire had a very interesting, and to me vital, commercial sideline. He sold, exchanged and recharged accumulator batteries. At home we did not have an electricity supply. Our lights were from paraffin lamps, static in the house and portable for the buildings, and our wireless (radio) required the resources of Mr Wiltshire's garden shed. As the power of the wireless battery failed, so the radio's sound volume got lower and lower, until it died. This event usually occurred when I wanted to listen to a world heavyweight boxing match commentated on by Raymond Glendenning with inter-round summaries by J Barrington Dalby. My first frustration with technology. Ear pushed against the speaker and pulse racing in direct disproportion to the failing sound.

Ossie was a different kettle of fish altogether. He was much older than the rest of us and had been kept back at the junior school over the leaving age of eleven years because he could not read. He was a bottom-ender and generally regarded as rough. I had been earmarked to help him read and because this seemed to be going well he made occasional visits to the farm. Normally, he would not have come close to this play circle. The big pay-off for me was protection. From the minute I started to help Ossie, it was clearly understood that it would not be a good idea to pick a fight with me. The brains for brawn trade-off.

What with new-found friends (bearing in mind the pre-five years had been absolutely isolated) and the farm as a playground and the Ossie protection, slowly the prison of school became more tolerable. Even so, I was always amongst the last to arrive in the morning and ran home as fast as my legs would carry me in the afternoon. I could never get home soon enough.

A few other things about Newton Primary School were both puzzling and fun. There were some good things about having other children around and it not being just me and the farm. Girls for a start. What do I make of these girls? Well, I arrive as an expert witness. A witness to temper, screaming, emotional blackmail, wanting her own way all the time and general nastiness. That is my sister. Some of her friends seem a bit better, none worse. Some wag once said that the big thing about men and women is that they are different. These girls were certainly different to me.

Perhaps because of my early years' experience with an elder sister, I was especially attracted to just a few girls due to them being so different. That is to say, cheerful, fun-loving, exciting and well, nice. I liked a girl called Margaret Riley who lived down Cragg Lane in Forge Cottage. I was always invited to her parties and was asked to sing and her mum made fantastic little cakes. Then there was Sandra Barlow who could wrestle on the playing fields as good as any lad and my special girl Audrey Spray. Audrey and I thought we might marry one day but we were beaten to it by a double wedding that took place one Saturday morning where the cobbler's path branched off from the path to Newton Old Hall. This posh event was supposed to be a secret but it seeped out and we all turned up to see the Collins sisters marry their respective boyfriends. Whether it actually legitimised anything, I never knew.

A few years later, there had been an outside chance that Mr George Alfred Smith (my dad) might really have slotted into the *haves* category in a non-too-fancy costume drama. He wanted to buy Newton Old Hall.

It must have been one of his rare, perhaps even sole and therefore unique, illusions of grandeur. It came on the market. I drove him to the Old Swan in Mansfield marketplace for the auction. Surprisingly it went for a very cheap price, far below the auctioneer's estimate, but as with the best beast at Chesterfield market, my dad remained silent. And in silent, and I suppose angry, frustration I helped him physically bump a car sideways that blocked our exit from that Old Swan car park.

The present Old Hall dates from about 1690 and was built in local stone. It was the squire in residence at that time who was registered on the title deeds as the original owner of Red Barn Farm. My dad had paid off the mortgage from the money received in compensation for the land lost to the M1, then en-route to Leeds. An earlier house on the same site as the Old Hall belonged to the Earl of Sheffield and it is possible for a building to have been there since Norman times when Newton was recorded in the Domesday Book. In the grounds of the Old Hall are three graves of a Mr Downing and his two wives. This arose due to the vicar of the day refusing to inter the Downings in the church yard because of Mr Downing's adultery. Mr Downing had married his wife's sister whilst his wife was still alive, although very ill and expected to die.

In the early nineteen hundreds, a family called Salmon liven in the Hall. One of the sons became Sir John and at one time was the first Air Marshall of the R.A.F. His brother, who was a naval officer, was killed in the First World War and had a military funeral from the Old Hall. Thus it was natural and poignant for the Mr Salmon, in residence at the time, to invite my dad and a few more men to walk from the George & Dragon one night to his home next door "to listen to the late news and see how our lads are getting on". That was during the Second World War and my sister and I had just appeared on the scene.

Games were another plus about Primary School. One can imagine all sorts of goings-on alone down the fields but for real games there are benefits from having some competition. Anyway, there wasn't a piece of ground flat and hard enough to play whip-and-top at home whereas at school it was possible to get the top all around the yard with practice and a clear run.

It was best to use a big fat top that had been chalked in circles to get the most colourful results whereas the slim tops known as window breakers were more likely to do just that long before the school yard circuit was complete. Similarly with marbles. If one's pocket money was saved to buy at least a few giant dobbers, then there was a huge advantage in holding one back for the final roll once all the others were down. Of course, if the dobber had to be played earlier, it presented a bigger target for the opponent to hit. Accuracy tinged with guile was the key to success.

It would be hard to over-praise the discipline of saving that prevailed in these early post-war years. Bearing in mind my dad never had any money (when he went out on a Friday night to "pay my club money" he would have to "see if mother has any change in her purse"), it must have been a big sacrifice to hand to both my sister and me a half-crown each week for the school savings scheme. It could equally have been a six-penny stamp that went into the savings book but our more brightly coloured stickers would eventually be handed in for a £5 sticker that covered the whole page. How we gloated over the gradual accumulation of these highly treasured pieces of paper. And what a prudential lesson for later life and a moral testament to the backbone that this country had after the horrors and depredation of those long war years. What a lesson in good parenting.

Nevertheless, there were still three enduring nightmares about these early school years. First was the mid-day dinner time. To most of the other boys it was obviously the best time. To me it was hell. The pre-cooked main meal arrived at the school in a large van, from where I never knew, and in metal trays. Almost always it consisted of some form of encrusted pie. This would be cut into squares by the dinner ladies and heaved onto the plate. If one was lucky, or unlucky, depending on how one viewed the pastry mound, the received item might be a corner piece. Successive ladies ladled out mashed potato, cabbage and most revolting of all, thick gravy. Always having had a poor digestive system, these dinners were either cause or effect. It's hard to say but, whatever, the smell alone made me heave.

Derbyshire boy

There was a boy called Alan Dillinger (not a farm-playing friend and very much a bottom-ender) who almost always received my pie dinner. He also regularly went back for seconds. Years later I saw him in a pub and marvelled with secret delight at his huge frame. It was the puddings that got me through. Once again, invariably a pastry pie but with some jammy type filling which, with custard, could be ingested. On extremely rare occasions, I even remember getting seconds.

But the real saviour was getting old enough to run fast enough to make it back home for dinner. Then it was always delicious hotpot. This of course was hot and since time was short the practice was to pick out the potato pieces and lay them along the edges of the bowl out of the stew liquid to cool. This worked because by the time the stew proper had been eaten with bread dropped in, the stranded potato pieces had cooled down. There must have been other dinners but only the hotpot is etched on a hungry brain.

The second really hateful aspect of early schooling, aside from the boring monotony of repetition, was the headmaster's obsession with football. He must have been obsessed because it was the only boys' game that was played and occupied just about every afternoon. I was hopeless. The sheer time absorbed must have gone some way to explaining why only those who were coached by school-teacher parents ever passed the 11+ and so via grammar school ever stood a realistic chance of an education. As an act of rebellious defiance, I never possessed a pair of proper football boots in my entire school life. My farming boots always sufficed.

Caning was the third big dread. It never happened to me but the Sword of Damocles was ever present. Certain troublemakers were perpetual recipients and one in particular learned to be so supple with his wrist that the angle from his extended arm almost reached the vertical. This clearly saved some pain from the form teacher that used a rounded ruler as the weapon. It did not however help much with the head teacher who cleverly used a bamboo cane with such a fast whip action as to defeat any small boy's antics. This particular child (Keith) took a massive revenge (aged ten). He set fire to the school of dreaded torture.

As to the lessons themselves, reading came quickly and easily. More surprising to me was how simple arithmetic was. I could not understand the problems most of the others had and just how slow they were. But never mind the lessons. Something much more interesting has happened. Our class of eight-to-nine year olds belonged to Miss Pollard who taught us for all subjects except football for boys and netball for girls. She was a very severe spinster and had been there so long that most of our parents had also been through her mill.

The memory-lodged incident occurred when a girl in the class reported to Miss Pollard that her Mars Bar had disappeared from her desk. On being asked to own up on three separate occasions during the last lesson of the day, the thief remained a mystery at going-home time. As a result, the redoubtable Miss Pollard was not going to let matters rest. We were all to stay behind "all night if necessary, and bringing in every child's parents if necessary" until the culprit came forward and handed back the Mars Bar or agreed to replace it. This overtime kangaroo court was particularly distressful for me because by this time my job was to run home and fetch the cows up the fields for milking and tie them up in the stalls. I was one of the first to start agitating for whoever did the deed to own up and let us go home. Child by child, Miss Pollard required each of us to stand up and relate in minute detail exactly what we had done at the afternoon playtime.

One boy started to cry quietly and visibly tremble at his desk. Miss Pollard went over to him, raised the lid of his desk and, inside, was the missing chocolate bar. This ranked amongst the most talked about events ever. Although not before this incident, this particular boy was to become a very good friend of mine and eventually an academic rival. Ironic that he was to break free from the secondary schooling dead-end and become very senior in a poacher turned gamekeeper way. So, skeletons in the cupboard from skeletons in the desk and soon to be skeletons in the fields.

Chapter two
Growing up

Because my sister was only sixteen months older than me and because she also had friends to play, there was at certain times some inquisitive horseplay between particular boys and particular girls. This would reach a head at haymaking time when the weather was warm, the new-mown grass soft and aromatic and there was a general air of high-spiritedness. It also seemed to coincide with my inability to get involved due to my job of loading the hay cart. Loading meant placing the hay (and in later years the hay bales) in an orderly manner on the cart from the disorderly way it was thrown up by pitch-forks from the hay-cocks that had been made to help the grass dry out and have some protection from the weather. As I grew stronger, my job developed into driving the tractor and pitching up the hay.

The trouble was, I enjoyed helping my dad and the hay had to be made and brought home to the stackyard, but at the same time, it prevented me from larking about with the girls and one boy in particular had a reputation for falling on top of a girl and staying there. Most of all I did not want this girl to be Audrey Spray particularly since I had noticed that this business of lying on top of a girl and not getting off seemed to make the girls as a whole like him more than any of the other boys. This was a subject of wonderment to me because in appearance he was quite ordinary. It also made me feel a bit strange and broke my concentration, I wanted to keep looking at what was going on instead of getting the hay straight on the cart.

In later life it occurred to me that a natural biological clock might run faster for certain individuals if they were destined for a short lifecycle. This advanced boy was to die young of multiple sclerosis. Short of things physical, experiments of a *look see* type between boys and girls down our fields were commonplace and appeared quite natural. Since after junior school and for the next six years or so I must have been too shy or introvert to have anything to do with girls, any thought of whether these little experiments came to be regarded as skeletons in the fields escaped me. Not that such thoughts haven't occurred since.

As time passed, the question of where babies came from started to arise and on this subject I was clear leader of the pack. My experiences allowed for an authoritative explanation of the reproductive process although this was never really believed. These experiences were based upon occasional trips with my dad to walk one of our two big white sows to a neighbouring farm that kept a boar for the specific purpose of breeding. Three things stuck in my mind about these quite long journeys across the fields. First, the sheer speed and willingness with which the sow made the outward journey, almost as if the purpose was both known and to be greatly enjoyed. Secondly, the length of time it took the boar to perform and the massive physical effort required of its owner to separate him from our animal. Thirdly, and most amazing of all, the vast amount of *spunk* that oozed from the sow during her long, slow and reluctant walk back home. It was incredulous to me that there would be any left to make the babies that were, after all, the only reason for the trip. This word for what the boar put into the sow was part of farming parlance and, because I was getting very interested in words at school, I had looked it up in our battered Chambers dictionary. Its prime definition of courage worked quite well with some of my compositions and so I used it, much to the acute embarrassment of two of my form teachers. One of these was the aforesaid Miss Pollard.

A further and similar experience of the worldly kind occurred much more frequently when one of our milking cows *in season* was taken to a nearer neighbour's bull. What struck me here was the difference from the pig in terms of speed and lasting interest. The bull required *one jump*, as it was referred to, and the owner always knew when this momentous event had occurred. Immediately the bull was led away seemingly now disinterested. This was in stark contrast to the boar and I immediately related the difference to the number of off-spring because for the cow there would be only one (on rare occasions two) but in the pig's case, many. Whether this observation about the quantity of offspring had any basis in fact, I never knew but I relayed it to my audience all the same. They still disbelieved.

The other experience I could relate was an everyday event in that my first job each morning was to let out the fowls. These fowls had been locked up each night in a big shed once they had roosted to prevent foxes from getting at them. The instant they emerged once the stone slab had been knocked away from the shed aperture, the cocks would engage in a veritable orgy of servicing the hens. It was the first priority above even eating. I knew that if this did not occur, the eggs would be infertile, should we want to get a broody hen to sit and hatch them. But again, I did not convince my friends who saw no connection with the matter of making babies. But I knew for sure and this made me superior. This blessing from being brought up on a farm and my dad having a business was to stay as setting me apart and being somewhat above them. The fact that we had very little in material terms did not enter into it.

Apart from the established job of fetching in the cows after school, there developed a host of tasks undertaken as a matter of course. Increasingly as time passed these jobs kept me distant from other children. This seemed to be a natural consequence of living down a long winding lane away from any other houses. My life was entirely with mum and dad and the farmyard, buildings, dog and cats, cows and pigs, fowls and ducks, the fields and the weather. I neither knew nor wanted anything else. School was a time-using nuisance and more and more the goings on of the other children outside school was of no interest.

The farm was not self sufficient as testament to the queuing for groceries at the co-op on Newton Green and the fortnightly visit from Bernard to take the cow cake, corn, crushed oats and flaked maze order. But it went a good way towards being independent. The garden saw to that. My dad was a good gardener of both vegetables and flowers. In reality he was probably better at gardening than farming and this was rare amongst the local farmers that I got to know.

So it was that on a Spring evening we started setting with the broad beans and early potatoes, then the small seeds of carrot, parsnip, swede, raddish, onion, lettuce and cabbage and moved on to planting the peas, until early May when it was safe from frost to put down the kidney beans. The methodology, resources and tools, and the growing and climbing aids employed, were second nature to me by the time I was eight years old. Not of course these terms. It was simply that I watched and copied, watched and copied. I still set in the same way today, no improvements have been forthcoming.

All this produce was for home consumption but there was one (gardening as distinct from farming) sales line. Blackcurrants. The queen of the soft fruit bushes bore a valuable harvest and we sold locally by the big black juicy pound. The value of vitamin C had been drummed home during the austere war years. There were plenty of takers and at a high price.

There were two other cash crops - field grown main-crop potatoes and hens' eggs. Potatoes grew well on my dad's heavy soil. The names of the varieties that did best became familiar, King Edward for red and Majestic for white and if there was a piece of new ground, then Duke of York could be tried. In the late summer the dried-off tops would be undermined by a cultivator drawn first by the horses and later by the grey Ferguson tractor. After the first hour or so the job of potato picking was arduous and backbreaking as the buckets having been filled were then emptied into sacks. Once the sacks were full they had to be heaved onto the cart and taken to the stackyard. Boys from the village were paid by the hour for the brief potato picking season and as with life's workers generally, some proved to be exceptionally good, others mediocre and the rest were rather slippery creatures.

The gathering-in was only part of the job to get the stuff to market. I worked with my dad on wet and cold autumn weekends to sort the potatoes into three groups. Good big ones for selling, medium grade for home use and *pig* potatoes. These latter small specimens would be boiled in an outside copper and later mixed with bran to feed the pigs as swill. Those potatoes selected as prime examples fetched a good price and were sold by the hundredweight sack in the village.

The hens provided the other cash crop. During the course of a week, the hens' eggs were collected from nesting boxes located in various places around the farm. Most were in the large fowl-shed in the orchard and I still itch when thinking about the visits to their flee-infested domain, although not on the wholesale scale occurring at the annual clean out. This full-day job would leave me covered in bites. My dad, alongside, was never touched. Strange.

Other nesting boxes were in the stables, cow shed and chamber. Some hens however would choose to lay where they wanted to and so a search of the stackyard and under the elderberry trees had to be undertaken. The big give-away of their hiding places was the cackling which accompanies the laying of an egg. When around at this time, a mental note of where this was taking place would be made for the collection job later.

This was not to say that a hen might not be successful in hiding her clutch of eggs. In such cases the evidence came to light later either in the form of a very happy hen appearing with her brand new family of chicks and for whom she would scratch around furiously, or on the discovery of an abandoned batch of eggs. In the latter case the trick was to put one egg in a bucket of water. If it floated, the eggs would be bad and my job was then to throw them all at the pig-sty wall as an act of enjoyable failure. It was interesting that the free-range hens and cockerels had no problem with consuming the stinking remnants. If the egg did not float then the batch would be taken indoors but put aside from the rest for home consumption *just in case*. This exercise was, of course, how I knew for sure about the consequences of the cockerels early morning activity.

All the eggs that had accumulated during the week had to be cleaned and crated on a Friday night. These eggs would be taken along with the milk churns to the village on the Saturday morning. My job, working in partnership with my dad, was to deliver these cleaned eggs by half-dozen or full dozen in a straw basket to the regular customers and collect the money. Sometimes, the regular customer had to be told that "this week there aren't any" because the number we had to sell was never consistent due to the weather, season, or simply because less than normal had been laid. Also, sometimes the price would be lower since the eggs were from pullets and smaller than normal.

When I first started delivering on my own, the customers were all relatives. This was easy and very welcoming although there was always the surprise that whilst I had been up and about for hours, these aunts and uncles were only just having breakfast and indeed sometimes actually waiting for me so they could add the eggs to their frying pan. At this time, we all had a cooked breakfast every morning.

As time passed, my customers grew to include non-family. With these I was much less happy. One house kept a bull-dog of which I was terrified, one family had a boy with an artificial (I think heavily skin grafted) face that I hated to see and another customer was stone deaf and I had great difficulty getting my money out of him. Blood out of a stone you might say.

Another regular job on the farm was fencing. This meant repairing or replacing the fences of the fields to stop the cows from breaking out into fields of growing crops or into neighbours' fields. Occasionally there would be an emergency. A cow or cows had broken through a fence and a gap had to be plugged. Routinely this was a Saturday afternoon job. The heavy cart was loaded with stakes, barbed wire, nails and staples and together with spades and heavy hammers the trip around the perimeter fencing would begin. This was tough and often quite treacherous work and one of the few times that gloves would be worn.

A further strong-man activity was muck-spreading. My role was to drive the tractor and due to the work being largely winter based and slow in execution, it was usually a cold experience not least because the Fergie 35 had no protection at all from the elements. All the filling of the cart and the spreading on the fields was manual, done by my dad with a fork and was very heavy and laborious work. My fondest memory when the muck had been spread and the cart was empty was the cue command "home James and don't spare the horses". My name was not James and we were not using horses!

A much more pleasant job was spudding. This had nothing to do with potatoes (which were colloquially known as spuds) and I never knew where the term came from but the tool was a narrow-bladed spade with a cut-out "v" shape on the top edge. The job was to dig out thistles from the meadow grass and because the intent was to do so before they seeded and thus spread, the job was deputed to me in the early Spring to early Summer season. My fondness for spudding came from picking a nice warm day and the immediate destruction of the thistle. However, the real treat was the isolation of the job. I loved being alone and attacking thistle after thistle. Gotcha, gotcha, great.

The meadow where most of the biggest thistles grew abutted the pit hills and the soil was poor because it had never been ploughed and fertilized. This in turn was due to the presence just below and just above the surface of foundation remains of the pit buildings. Beneath one stone slab was a deep well and jumping up and down on that stone was irresistible. The pit had ceased working in about 1890.

This meadow was known as Deadwater and the stream running alongside to join the county boundary stream was

Deadwater Brook. I was told from an early age that it acquired this name due to a tragedy in the mid 1800's when a young girl was seen walking down our lane and continuing towards the pit carrying a bundle in her arms. Because she was seen returning without the bundle, a search revealed a drowned baby in the pit pond located in that meadow fed by that brook. A sad pedigree for a beautiful peaceful place.

The next field along was known as the Wharf. This was because along its straight narrow length was a raised edge that had once carried railway truck rails. Horses pulled coal trucks from the pit some five miles to Pinxton Wharf from where the canal system eventually fed the river Trent. Industry comes and industry goes. Today those fields remain the same although light industrial buildings creep closer and closer and traffic from the M1 is just audible. But it was very quiet when I spudded and picked violets to take home.

A dual activity as heavy and physical as muck spreading was hedging and ditching. It shared the late autumn and early winter season and I was little more than an observer. Ditching in particular was incredibly tough and slow work and the main tool was a spade with an elongated head with turned- in sides. Its purpose was to get depth in heavy clay-based soil at the edge of each field to drain off surplus water. This was work for a strong man. That same man would wield a long-handled hedge knife to pare down the season's growth to layer at about a 45 degree angle. This process that we called pleaching produced a thick hedge for the next year. Even today whenever I see a pleached hedge I never fail to admire this age-old practice with nostalgic pangs. Smallholding farmers such as my dad had to be strong, skilful and multi-tasked, though I never knew it at the time.

Because it didn't start until well into December, went on throughout the winter and was prevented only by the tractor and trailer being bogged down in the mud, turnip-pulling and gathering-in was the consistently coldest occupation. Gloves were never worn. Instead, the swinging of both arms across the chest to bash against the rib-cage like some demented scarecrow was the practised method of getting some feeling back into the fingers. Then would follow hot-aches (terrible pains as blood rushed back into the fingers) and a re-start to work. The process was simple enough in that a turnip (actually a swede) pulled from the soil and held in the left hand was separated from its green leafy top by a swipe of the evil looking curved turnip knife. The root was allowed to drop to the left and the greenery thrown to the right. Since the next row was pulled whilst walking in the opposite direction, it followed that two rows of produce and tops were available for collecting later. These turnips were hand thrown into a cart and taken to the farmyard for pitting, that is, put into one big pile on which straw and then soil was laid as a protection from frost.

A never-ending chore from this point until the cows were turned out in mid- April was the collection of turnips from the pit to be placed into the turnip grinder. At first turned by hand, and later by a small machine, the grinder reduced the vegetable to slivers for shovelling into the cow troughs as winter feed. When I was aged three, it also reduced the large finger of my left hand by about an inch when my internal inquisitiveness went unnoticed by a small helper. A *rushed* trip by horse and cart and then bus to Chesterfield Royal Hospital restored the figure end but the resultant shape at the tip of this big finger and the scar are testimony to the excitement. There seemed to be lots of lurking dangers for a growing boy getting involved at that time although I had to wait until aged ten before falling off the top of the hay cart and sustaining what I was proud to repeat as a greenstick fracture. My pot arm lasted for six weeks.

The turnip grinder went round in circles just as the future will have the workers going round. When I was still very young, we had a lodger. He was a star. A Polish star. A refugee from the war, Stan (his real name was unpronounceable) got a job working on the coal face but he helped my dad with the hard physical side of the farm, voluntarily. At haymaking he was the fastest and the strongest but best of all he took me to the picture palace in Newton and bought me toffee to eat during the film. Stan was my best grown-up friend at the time and I admired his hard working attitude, his efforts at improving his English and the fulfilment of his promise to get me some real Polish stamps for my collection. They kept coming and coming. I had the best collection in the whole school of these strange stamps with their agricultural scenes. Now, through the European Union, the Stans are back with us and it is bad news for Poland as it is good news for us. Our Stan, like so many of his compatriots, went to America to find a permanent new life. Good luck to Stan and to all the new Stans.

Not all the refugees left or went back home. In Newton we had Nicky a Ukrainian who integrated fully and for whom my dad often did some ploughing. Nicky was a very respected citizen and liked his pint in the George & Dragon. He bought a house and married and lived a long life in this backwater that, one assumes, had the great merit of safety first.

But the start of the agricultural revolution, even in placid middle England, had been far from safe. The trigger had been the unveiling in 1778 of a prototype *threshing machine.* Invented by the Scottish millwright Andrew Meikle, both the first and then a second version failed. However, as with all mothers of invention, a mechanical method had to be found to separate the wheat from the chaff. The back-breaking work of farmers beating their grain with sticks or ropes to knock the seeds from the stalks simply could not keep pace with the rapidly growing population.

Meikle's third machine consisted of a strong drum with fixed wooden arms that beat the corn rather than just rubbed it as in his two failed attempts. Although this threshing machine was eventually a huge success it received a stormy reception from farm workers. Like many labour-saving devices designed during the period, it threatened livelihoods and machines were often set fire to by angry workers. Things came to a head in 1830 in what became known as the Swing Riots. But it was too late and the effort to stave off mechanisation was in vain. The threshing machine soon became a common sight throughout the countryside.

Initially powered by horse and then steam engine, Fred Ball's huge beast of a threshing machine that struggled down our winding lane in late autumn was driven by his big Fordson Major tractor. Of course, its actual operation now was relatively safe as certain guards had been fitted to moving parts and other potentially lethal apertures had been blocked off. But, the main reason for the dramatic reduction in the horrendous accidents that occurred in earlier times was that by this stage tap water was clean and, more specifically, home brewed tea made from that water could be given to the men safely. The only safe way to quench the thirst of sweating men in 1850 was to give them ale and lots of it, six or seven pints a day of it. Some farms even had their own brewery. Men in ale make mistakes.

Threshing day was the biggest day of the farming calendar. If the stacks of corn, wheat and oats – the land wasn't good enough for barley – were left too long then the rats and mice would have a field day. Therefore, to get an early booking for Fred Ball was very important. Not that my dad had much pulling power relative to the bigger men. Fred would arrive with two and sometimes even three of his own men. Such men travelled with Fred for the season and were paid by him and became part of the contracted cost of threshing. Always there would be Little Joe but the others varied. Little Joe had a specific job. He fed the sheaves of corn into the drum and so spent the day on top of the monster machine and knew exactly at what pace to feed the beast.

The large tractor was fitted with a special spindle that rotated with the engine power and in turn drove belts attached to the threshing machine. Once the various cogs and wheels started to turn, there was no stopping it. The big threshing day had begun. My dad usually threw corn sheaves from the stack to the top of the machine to a man who cut the string and passed on to Little Joe to feed the drum. At first, this job of handling the stacked sheaves (later to be my job) was easy since the throwing was downhill but then a critical point was reached. As the stack of sheaves got lower so the throwing became uphill and consequently much harder. It was particularly hard near the base of the stack, first because of the height to throw the sheaves, secondly the compactness of the stack and thirdly to avoid the rats and mice scurrying for safety. Not that the rodents escaped, the dogs and cats saw to that. A dog kills a rat in a special way. It throws it in the air and catches it when it falls. Cats have more stealth. It pays to learn to distinguish between dogs and cats.

Threshing day was a labour-intensive day. Many more men than Fred brought with him were actually needed. Such extra hands came from neighbouring farms on a quid pro quo basis. They gave a day's labour in return for my dad going to help on their own big day. It was a system that worked well and was traditional and was itself much discussed around the dinner table. Not least what the host farmer's wife had fed them. At certain places like Red Barn Farm a full roast dinner with apple pie to follow was routine but not all wives were like Mary. Some struggled to serve up cheese and pickle. This information was fascinating to me as was Fred telling the assembled group that in relation to women generally "all mares are much the same when saddle comes off." An expression that puzzled me for years.

Haymaking was the most magical time. This was probably because it signalled the start of summer and a new farming season. This joy though was always tempered in my mind by the worry of whether, once we got started, there would be enough dry days strung together to allow the hay to form without damage from rain. If it did rain, how much damage would be caused by the constant knocking about as the outdoor drying processes took place? Another knock-back for me was the frustration of knowing that things would not be ready.

Even though a late June to early July start was a virtual certainty, it would always come to light that some essential part was needed for the mowing machine and that the only answer was to get the blacksmith in the next village of Tibshelf to make it. Since this was not his proper job and since he had had no notice, there was no certainty when it might be ready and if it would work. Even on the first day of haymaking the mowing knife would not have been sharpened and my dad would start a search for the one used last year and for the back-up spare. Even when located (probably in its wooden box tied round with binder twine and hanging from a rafter in the Chamber) there was always the chance that it would need repairing (maybe welding) and at a minimum some of the blades would need replacing or re-riveting.

Once all this reparation had been achieved and invariably having lost three or four good sunny days, the sharpening process was neither easy nor quick. Each knife consisted of many triangular blades riveted to a metal arm that had to fit into the mowing machine bed. The two edges of each triangle had to be sharpened and so, with twenty or so blades, this was a major job. Also, and depending upon the condition and type of grass being mown, the knife as a whole needed re-sharpening periodically. This is where the spare came into play if mowing was to carry on. From my perspective all these potential snags got in the way of doing the best job possible. It was also the most essential job because without hay to feed the cows during the winter (turnips and kale and cabbage being only supplements) there would be little or no milk and with no milk my dad had no income. Perhaps my business brain was forming. My dad saw no such need for urgency, pre-planning and preparation.

He continued to scratch a living for a further 35 years from 35 acres of undulating poor coal-infested soil until the day he died, having just collected the eggs.

Chapter three
Square peg – round hole

In truth, my dad had too good a brain to be a small farmer. He had, however, no choice. Born the next to youngest of seven in a terraced house on Littlemoor Lane (and therefore a top-ender), he had been moved to Red Barn Farm at the age of twelve to live with his paternal grandmother following the death through cancer of his mother aged 50. Eight years later, his father was killed aged 59 by a fall of clay at the nearby clay pits where he worked. In that same year (1935) his grandmother died aged 94 "having never had a day's illness in her life. She often drank the milk after it had gone sour and I've seen her pick maggots out with a kitchen knife from the meat hanging in the dairy before eating the meat. Didn't seem to do her any harm". My dad often told me that an hour before she died she asked to see him whilst lying in bed in the front room and said "George I'm going now, look after the farm and be a good boy".

So, at the age of twenty-one, he was left alone to run the tenanted farm just as he had been told. The farmhouse and a few surrounding acres that were called the back field had actually been purchased years before by his grandfather and the rest of the land was taken on later as a tenancy from Chatsworth Estate (the seat of the Duke of Devonshire). His grandfather had clearly been a man of some ability having risen from being a miner to a mining contracts manager who ran contracts for the pit owner, employed the men directly and participated in profits. He had died a man of substance owning not only the farmhouse and adjacent land but also a row of houses in the bottom end of the village as well as two or three in the top end. He was born in 1843 and sired 10 children the youngest of which was my Great Aunt Pem. His name was John Smith.

Having left the village school aged fourteen, I feel sure my dad harboured a secret ambition to get a proper if late education. In his teens he had cycled, during several winters, to night-school in the village of Heanor which was at least ten hilly miles away. He must have studied mathematics because I still have his textbooks on geometry and trigonometry. Why this led to nowhere I never knew.

Perhaps it was as compensation that he took to reading. In those early days I would meet him once a fortnight after school at the mobile library where he would hand in a shopping bag full of books and replenish them. I cannot remember what type of material he went for but a book would go up the stairs to bed with him at night and in the morning it was read. There were perhaps two pointers. He quoted Shakespeare often and when the trips to the mobile library finished, a large book in the cabinet in the front-room, H E Bates – Short Stories, was taken out over and over again.

Certainly he was intellectually frustrated and spent this angst in deliberately picking an argument on some emotionally charged subject. Usually this peaked with his elder sister and her family at a traditional Boxing Day tea. The perfect trigger would be an inevitable reference at some stage in the proceedings to the Royal Family. My dad's stock response that always precipitated our departure, to my mother's disgrace, was "Line 'em all up against a wall and shoot the buggers".

For a man who lived, one would have thought, a physical, outdoor and therefore healthy life, my dad had been fortunate to live beyond his early forties. He had a very serious illness. It started with boils appearing on his arms that developed multi-heads and turned into carbuncles, the likes of which I have never heard of or seen since. These ugly menacing extrusions were being treated with poultices by Doctor Graham at his surgery in Tibshelf. But then came the devastating headaches. He was in great pain and took to walking the kitchen with his head in his hands and one day I saw him bang his head against the solid stone wall. The biggest wonder was that he did not kill himself.

For the first time ever, my dad could not handle the farm. He could not even walk outside to fetch the cows for milking. There was not the slightest possibility of him actually milking the cows, and cows have to be milked twice a day. My mum called on the help of her family even though he would not have wanted this to happen. He was a proud man and secretive of his routines but there was no choice but to take the help.

Uncle Ernie came from Sherwood Street and brought his son Edwin and Uncle Eric came from his butchery shop in Sutton. From my dad's side of the family, Uncle Harold came from Sutton just as he had always done. The Wilsons, my mum's side, thought Uncle Harold was slow and told him so. Well, slow he might have been but he was consistent and reliable and plodded on helping at the farm for many more years. The Wilsons proved to be an emergency one-off event. Buried within this recollection is a little lesson.

The headaches were eventually diagnosed as internal boils. Really? Had the cause been far worse, the rest of this story would have been much changed. The farm was my dad. Without him.......

My dad becoming 50 years old was concurrent with my younger brother, Alan, leaving school and the farm income reducing to a pittance. He took a big decision. Rather than Alan having to find a job, he would let him stay with the animals and he (now to be known as George) would go out into the big wide world instead. It was a magnanimous gesture for which he was never repaid. He took a job in the cable-shop at the pit "my first pay packet". He was put on days but he also worked on the night-shift and the job lasted until he retired at age 65. To my eyes this was a very sad come-down but he did enjoy the company of the other men and they seemed to take to him judging from the greetings in the local pub on occasional Sunday lunchtimes. "Farmer George" he was called, almost as if to reinstate the lost status.

My dad being on someone else's payroll could have happened much earlier. When I was seven years old and with him looking at some young beast kept in a building 100 yards remote from the farmyard and known as the hovel, he suddenly turned to me for a serious talk. He explained that within the last year the seventh Duke of Devonshire had died leaving substantial death duties to be paid. To meet these liabilities, the succeeding Duke had decided to sell off much of the tenanted farm acreage including our farm. There were two options. Either we leave and he got an employed job somewhere (which he explained my mum would prefer) or he attempted to raise a mortgage from the National Westminster Bank to purchase the land at a preferential price as offered to the sitting tenant. I may have been only seven but the thought of leaving hit me like a kick from one of our horses, as he would have known it would. I said he should try to buy the land. I think he needed the confidence of the two-to-one vote that he had been certain to get.

That little chat condemned my mum, who was about to give birth to a third child and had miscarried two years earlier, to a life of some considerable isolation and for many years not much comfort. But how was I to know and what would the alternative have been? I didn't even know she had come from a successful family of butchers with a large spacious house and most of the amenities the times had to offer. I didn't know she married at 21 to a tenant farmer of poor soil and a house lacking electricity, proper mains water, water closets (toilets) and which would be so damp over enough years to bring on the *rheumatics*.

Still, it was the start of the strongest possible bond with my dad and it did cause me to help him as much as I could so the mortgage could be paid and we could keep our farm. That my mum spent every Monday in the washhouse with no machinery at all and the rest of the days cleaning, cooking, caring and slaving was just one of those things. That she got jobs like dashing down the yard from the dairy with a bowl of warm fresh pig's blood stirring rapidly to avoid it clotting before adding pearl barley and whatever else was needed to produce black pudding, was all part of the contract. That she was saddled with nursing a sickly child (me) with constant trips to the doctors, and the seemingly endless waits for our turn, for him to once again stick some horrible needle type instrument into my ear in an attempt to solve the unfathomable problem of my near constant earache. That she sat through my nightmare rantings of seeing strange objects threaded to the edge of the blankets and then to face another day when I hadn't, again, gone to the toilet but had had bad indigestion and felt very sick. And why should this be when my dad could eat a raw Spanish onion with a stick of celery and freshly pulled radishes on the side, just before going to bed? All this in the days when ignorance was bliss on the need for roughage foods, and the non-need for fatty foods such as the suet dumplings, and when temperature control for fevers was ill-understood. All this, and more, was part of my mum's contract.

She who was such a natural mother with her deep   breathing as she ascended the winding stairs to check if my sister and I were asleep. She who would like to have gone with her husband to the dances held at the church hall in the winter months, but my dad didn't do that sort of thing. He didn't buy her birthday presents either. Nor did he agree with the request (made personally on a special visit to the farm by the headmaster) during my first year at secondary school for me to be transferred to William Rhodes School at Chesterfield that held open some places for the likes of myself. It seems I came top in a maths exam set for all years from age eleven to fifteen. The Mars Bar boy went instead.

It is a truism that whether one endures a distasteful phase with acquiescence, or by kicking and knocking over the traces, it passes. If you have reached eleven years of age and have failed the 11 plus exam then a shift to the big Secondary Modern school is enforced. It might only be three miles or so away but its huge size and mixture of children from six villages the size of mine and numerous tiny hamlets, made it a fabulous new world. The one thing that started to boost my confidence was that we learned from day one that each new intake had been pre-graded. Our first form class was to be 1A, 1B, or 1C. How this decision had been arrived at I never knew nor cared because I was in 1A. Furthermore, after a series of tests on different subjects it appeared I was either top of the class or number 2. Although my aptitude was reckoned to be with figures, the English teacher had, after one of these initial tests, made me stand at the front and explain to the others what the word mortgage meant. This I proceeded to do with great assuredness. Of course no-one including Mr Finney knew how I had acquired this advanced knowledge.

To me, the big difference in the learning stakes from the junior school was that at the end of each lesson we moved physically to another classroom for the next subject. This was a rock-solid guarantee that in the, let's say, history room, would be a teacher who knew everything there was to know about history and the classroom would be bedecked with history charts and related material and the books would be dedicated solely to history. I thought that this was magical and it started to occur to me that there existed many areas of knowledge that were not related to each other and that any one of these could be explored in depth. The time blocked off in the schedule of lessons for geography had a particular thrill. I loved hearing about foreign places and memorising their locations and was soon badgering my favourite uncle for one of his old atlases.

This uncle became a very special person in my early thirst for knowledge. Having married one of my dad's elder sisters (in fact the sister my dad used to taunt on Boxing Day and any other day he got the chance) he worked in a library from a very early age and eventually become chief librarian of three local centres. He had a quiet cultured disposition and at this stage of my early years, would come to the farm every Wednesday and Saturday afternoon. These were his two half days off and he came specifically to help my dad on the farm. He travelled always by bus and walked the last mile or so across the fields.

Uncle Harold was a boundless source of knowledge. He named wild flowers that had not been known to us and when it got dark early under a clear sky, and we went back down to the fields to burn thorns from the hedge-cutting of earlier in the day, he would look up and point out the main star constellations. Whilst I have recognised the main ones ever since "and look along the line of the last two stars of the bucket of the Plough – keep going and there is the bright North Star – you will never lose your direction if you can find the North Star", the cluster he pointed out that I have never heard mentioned since was "the Red Indian Eye Test". He said there were 24 stars in the tightly bunched pack. The number that could be counted determined the quality of eyesight. I could never see more than about 12 and so concluded that I would have made a poor Indian brave.

When my sister and I were very young, he always brought the Dandy and Beano comics, "last week's issue from the library". Later on he brought me the Hotspur, Wizard and the Eagle because they contained proper stories. Later still he brought library books - White Fang by Jack London, Tom Sawyer, Huckleberry Finn, Biggles and this was why at Tibshelf Secondary Modern I was an avid listener above the desk lid and an avid reader below. Agatha Christie, J B Priestly, the adventures of Captain Hornblower, it went on and on.

Uncle Harold told me about his holidays, walking in the Highlands of Scotland, on Arran and in the Shetlands and Orkneys. I positively ached to do the same someday. By the year of his death, 1967, he had spent 42 years in the library service. At the funeral service at Teversal church, the vicar described him as "well-read, filled with erudition, filled with kindliness and firm but companionable". I could have added that he was my best grown-up friend and teacher and brought bones for our dog every Saturday, except that I couldn't because, although 25 by then, I was too choked to speak. From letters written to the local paper along with the funeral report it turned out that he had been the founder member and first president of Sutton and District Rambling Club. There was a reminder too that he introduced the winter lectures and I recall vividly the one given by Percy Edwards the bird whistler. And that's another easily forgotten lesson, how to recognise the whistles and calls of the many different birds in the fields and stackyard and do not forget also that a member of the finch family can always be recognised because it flies in bursts not continuously. I owed him so very much.

If geography became a favourite by interest, so English language did by effort. At first my spelling was abysmal but gradually and probably through reading it started to improve. It was when the zenith of 16 out of 20 was reached that a realisation dawned that there must somehow be rules, must be something useful in grammar that hitherto had been unbelievably dry and abstract. As I started to unravel the structure of sentences, detect the adjective, noun, pronoun and verb, so the rules of spelling started to make sense and if just exceptions accounted for the 4 out of 20 I got wrong then it felt an achievement.

Looking back, there must have been much self-deception about this but still it propelled me forward and English grew closer to maths in the ability stakes. Added to this, there was something gloriously unstructured about the English lessons. Mr Finney was thought to have been ticked-off by the headmaster for having been spotted reading to us when we should have been working. Yet, his passion for Robert Louis Stevenson's Travels with a Donkey stay with me to this day as it is spotted on special offer in a shop in Barcelona and was this, even if subconsciously, the linkage of the very separate subjects of English, geography and history? Special offer though, says it all.

Whatever the merits of how English was taught, my confidence grew perceptively and when in the fourth year he asked me to be the assistant editor of the school magazine and awarded a special prize for my efforts (Doctor in the House and Doctor at Sea), the seeds of a lifelong interest in words were well and truly sown. It's strange to look back on this hater of institutionalised junior school, the one who got there last and who couldn't wait to get back home, the lonesome always introvert non-joiner of any team thing, actually being presented on the annual prize-giving day with The Cruel Sea credit prize 2nd boy in second year and Atomic Energy first prize 1st boy in 3rd year. The date of the ceremony for the fourth and final year was never reached and there would be no call back. I left school on my fifteenth birthday and started work the following day.

It's one thing to find an interest and to want to work at it, quite another to have to do things for which one has no aptitude, zero interest, and can see no sense in spending time at. Woodwork and metalwork were not only compulsory but took up the whole of one afternoon a week when things should have been, and needed to be, learnt. Here I was firmly in the C category and never graduated from soft to hard wood and was only let loose on metalwork at all because it appeared that some time had to be devoted to this harder discipline irrespective of the progress, or lack of it, at woodwork.

The abject failures still haunt me. A wooden toy boat, the first and most basic article, that sank instantly. The coffee table that was proudly presented to my Great Aunt Pem (many lessons after the rest of the class had moved on to more advanced things) and the legs of which broke as soon as she put some magazines on it. It nevertheless stayed in her parlour semi-propped up. The metal fish-slice complete with holes that my mum kept in her cutlery drawer to the very end even though the rivets were obviously out of line and it was branded with the number 15, my role number in the ill-fated class, that I assume should never have been there in the first place.

Whilst the rest of the class turned out innumerable multi-grained fruit bowls, my single product looked like something dropped from outer space. Even my mum never really took to it. The same teacher who supervised these two vital crafts also took practical science and consequently was completely unmoved on the afternoon that a bunsen burner conspired to singe the hair on the front of my head.

Sports absorbed about as big a proportion of the timetable as it had unfortunately done at junior school. All activities were highly competitive and came to a public head at the annual sports day held at a municipal facility some distance from the school that had no field of its own. The competitive spirit was generated by the clever trick of dividing us up into four houses. At the great annual event, each house collected points in each year according to the positioning of the child in a race. The allocation to a house was permanent and so lasted for the whole four years. It was supposed to be somehow fair and equal although the selection method was never clear and if it was, why did the winning points tally always seem to follow the known importance of the Derbyshire house in question such that Chatsworth (blue) invariably came first, Hardwick (red) second, Haddon (green) third and Wingfield Ruin (yellow) last. I was in Wingfield. Whilst I did have some minor success in two areas, both were attributable to my upbringing and in no way any coaching on offer.

The first was cricket. On some Saturday evenings in the summer and going back as far as I can remember, a game of cricket was organised. It took place in the field below the stackyard using hay pegs for wickets and bails, and a home-made bat, until Uncle Harold's son Philip appeared one glorious day with a proper bat that had three springs. I was allowed to use this super bat provided the ball was hit properly in the middle of the bat and not too hard.

There was no team but whoever made the most runs was the winner. Usually there were only three players, Uncle Harold, Philip and me. Very occasionally and when he was not too busy after milking the cows, my dad would be persuaded to take part. He had a most strange way of bowling and this baffled me such that I rarely managed a proper hit. My superior knowledge now suggests that he was a form of leg spinner. The one advantage that was derived from these enjoyable evenings was the absolute necessity on my part to bowl like a veritable demon if Philip with his new proper bat was ever to be dislodged. Of-course, the bumpy surface of the meadow helped as did the occasional cowpat. This grounding could well have produced the next in a long line of Derbyshire fast bowlers for county and England. Instead it produced an opening bowler for Wingfield at the rarely held school-year team match with a local rival. I cannot recall a single victory but only taking a blinding catch once at cover-point. It must have been so because it got a special mention by the headmaster at school assembly the following morning.

The second claim to fame arose undoubtedly from the routine run down the fields to fetch up the cows for milking or the emergency run to recapture a cow that had broken out into a neighbour's field. It so happened that Tibshelf Secondary Modern had a similar obsession as Newton Junior with football, or perhaps a sports master who neither wanted nor knew any other winter sport. Whatever the cause, my anti-campaign was to continue - still no boots and still a disposition to shoulder-charge or deliberately trip any opposing forward heading in my direction. As a result, those who would never make any of the football teams were no longer required to turn up. Instead and on each football afternoon we would go on a long-distance run. This was fine in its way except that first there was no sports master to supervise, guide, or otherwise instruct and secondly there was no actual course to run.

Having no course was solved by someone suggesting that we take one of two alternate routes each week. The first was from school to the nearby village of Morton and back. This was all on the road. The second and much longer run was to Hardwick Hall and back a distance of about five miles partly on the road and partly across fields by footpath. It is strange to think that all we abandoned football drop-outs could easily have got out of sight of school and generally messed about. Yet, a kind of unvoiced competitiveness set in. Most actually did try to run as fast as possible and an elite few proved to have more stamina than the others. These budding marathon athletes, that included me, were all wiry and skinny whilst the ones who trailed behind were mostly fat. After a while, my superior stamina for the longer distance was being challenged by just one boy.

How weird that this John Smith*son* was born ten days after me, surely too soon to be my son! be a Newton bottom-ender of all things and not someone with whom I had previously been friends. Nevertheless, our solitary running battles started a friendship that would last to this day and his ability to smoke a surreptitious fag amazes me as much now as then. Whether under the stone bridge that carried the railway line over Morton, or resting on the fallen oak tree up the hill into Hardwick Hall park, he would produce from heaven knows where secreted on his skinny running-top-and-shorts dressed person, a single Park Drive cigarette and from somewhere else a single match which when struck on a stone created the contented smoker. I knew of no one else this young who had started to smoke and I was to hold off this manly habit until I was well over sixteen years of age.

It was around this time that my second source of income arose. My aunt Gladys had arrived at the farm one day carrying a large box containing several bantam chicks (banties). She had been instructed to bring them by her husband uncle Leslie for me because they were a very special breed that I was to look after. She explained that they were Polish Tufted banties that he had acquired as eggs from Nottingham University's experimental department and that he had used one of his own broody hens to hatch the eggs. Although uncle Leslie worked for British Railways as a painter of signal boxes and the like, he had a part-time job in the evenings and some nights as a caretaker and watchman for the university, the grounds of which abutted their garden.

Quite what went on in this experimental department it never occurred to me to ask and even if I had, the probability is that he either wouldn't have known or told. Still, these most unusual chicks arrived complete with little tufts on their heads and the first tiny evidence of spikes on the rear of the legs of those destined to be cocks. Seeing these miniature fowls gave me an idea. I approached my dad with a proposition. If they were to become my sole responsibility as regards building special coops to hold them away from the rest and keep them clean and manage the breeding, would he supply the same corn and other food as the main flock had and could I then keep any money that was forthcoming from the sale of the eggs? To my relief this deal was agreed.

It followed that in due course there were banty eggs collected, cleaned, crated and ready to sell. At first the selling was not as easy as I had thought since the regular customers, as always, had proper full-sized eggs, sometimes the bonus of a double-yoked one, and were even prone to complain if they believed too many white eggs had been mixed with the preferred brown ones. However, my sales pitch had three planks to it. First, the audience was largely a captive one consisting in the main of my aunts, secondly the price was less at four shillings a dozen as distinct from six shillings for the hen eggs and the coup-de-grace was my heart-felt knowledge imparted to them with great sincerity that once cracked into the frying pan, the size was hardly any less than a hen's egg.

Once the banty eggs started to get larger as I augmented my small flock of Polish Tufted with other strains, the sideline proved a winner. Now I had my second income stream to add to Great Aunt Pem's weekly pocket money for the chores. Also, and although it wasn't obvious to me in a technical sense at the time, the distinction between revenue and capital cash spend became important. The only means available to buy more birds and in pursuit of which I avidly scoured advertisements in the Derbyshire Times, was to save some of the egg money. And so a good business lesson was learned.

Capital is an investment for the future and short of borrowing, current income must be set aside. Also, to have to borrow like my dad's mortgage would mean paying interest and no one else was going to have a slice of my profit. My dad got his own back from providing the feed in that about 50% of new chicks would turn out to be cock birds and because a ratio of only about one to ten was needed to keep the eggs fertile, fully grown males were killed for eating. I was assured that they were too small to sell and so they entered the farm food chain and usually for a Sunday lunch.

A few years later and again by pure chance I was to start bell-ringing and it was only after a good deal of proficiency had been attained that the invitations started to arrive to ring for the wedding on Saturday. Now here was a real money-spinner because the fee per bell was substantial and there were no costs at all just a modest amount of personal time. A sure omen for a slice of the future in consultancy.

Aunt Gladys was my favourite aunt. She was the third eldest on my dad's side of the family and like most girls at that time had gone into service on leaving school. That was a polite expression for becoming a servant of a wealthy family. She had started a somewhat unusual and thereafter fairly eccentric life after her early working years by marrying Uncle Leslie who already had a daughter by his first wife who had died very young. She had inherited money on her father's death before she was thirty and had bought a house on the west side of Nottingham and invested and hung on to the rest.

The couple had a highly charged but close relationship that became familiar to my sister and me from an early age because of the custom that developed over a few years of fetching us to stay with them for two weeks in the summer to give my mum and dad a break on their own. It was a world vastly different from the farm. They lived on a street with semi-detached neighbours in a densely built-up area on the fringe of the city. Consequently, people and noise bamboozled me.

Aside from the environmental aspect, my mum and dad were quiet and, apart from on just two occasions, lived at peace with each other. This was not the case during our holiday. Aunt Gladys was a large lady abounding with household energy. As she charged around and most obviously when she rushed to the front door, the whole house seemed to shake and certainly the floorboards did. Uncle Leslie was also dynamic in a less noisy way but the really frightful new experience was their arguments. It was as if anything could trigger one off and once on a bus coming back from Nottingham Slab Square it happened over which was the nearest bus stop to alight for their house. Apart from the fact that they had lived there long enough to have measured it out to the inch if it was important, it was, to my sister and me, completely baffling in that either of the two options were very close and no distance at all compared with the walks to and from school that we did quite thoughtlessly each day. This particular and public bust-up so upset my sister that she refused to go on holiday to their place ever again - and didn't.

Having a childhood punctuated by no more than two parental arguments must be a rarity and maybe for this very reason are remembered for their devastating effect as utter surprises. One arose when after an afternoon's milking session, my dad could not find any filter papers. These papers were placed between two metal discs, themselves filled with tiny holes, and literally filtered the milk as it was poured from the milking bucket before being cooled and entering the churn. Without being filtered, the milk could not therefore be made ready for collection by the dairy lorry. For some inexplicable reason the misunderstanding about whether my dad or mum should have fetched a new supply of these filters developed into a full-scale argument. And, for the first and only time, it became clear that mum not only knew how to swear but could deliver a certain word to great and loud impact. We were shocked and frightened and it was obviously my dad who was backing off. When things quietened down my mum in a low and sweet voice started to sing over and over again and to herself a rhyme that I had never heard before or indeed since and have no inkling of its origin:-

We're miserable, so miserable, down on misery farm
The hens won't lay
We can't make hay
We work all day and get no pay
We're miserable, so miserable, down on misery farm

The second altercation must have occurred in the early hours of one New Year's Day after being woken by a huge noise downstairs and creeping half way down the winding staircase to explore, it appeared that my dad's attempt to *let in the new year* had gone badly wrong and mum was shouting at him and he was falling all over the kitchen and bumping into chairs and the table. Only years later did realisation dawn that he had been the worse for drink and on being pressed my uncle Ernie admitted that he and his son Edwin and a few others may have "spiked your dad's beer to send him on his way". Years later still, a photograph emerged of my dad with a pint in one hand and a cigarette in the other and taken in the upstairs room at the George and Dragon pub in the village.

For a virtual non-drinker and only an occasional pipe smoker, it must have been quite a night and not one my mum was likely to let him forget. The only other thing I can actually recall of the incident at the time, was his great difficulty in milking the following morning on account of "my bad head" and my mum "having to do a lot of cleaning up".

What made Uncle Leslie so different was that he kept cage birds for a hobby. Perhaps hobby is the wrong perspective since he traded these birds and had many stories of his financial success in this regard. Such successes were invariably challenged by Aunt Gladys on the basis of "and who bought them and fed them?" Whilst this was usually voiced with a laugh for my benefit, it could lead to a major argument that to me was very upsetting.

The birds were kept in the garden in huge wire cages attached to sheds and all of which he had built himself. These constructions went around all three fences of the back garden with more down the middle. There were also many small cages in the kitchen and in a conservatory. He also kept tropical fish in innumerable tanks and had several ponds in the garden where special forms of flies were bred for their eggs to feed the fish. In his later years when the house was sold for a retirement place, and although the birds were all disposed of, some fish tanks remained and were re-installed in the new abode. As I grew older it became apparent that this hobby stemmed from a deep-seated interest and considerable ornithological knowledge. The loss of his birds must have been a mortal blow.

As well as the more common birds such as canaries, budgerigars and Java sparrows others that stick in my mind with great affection were the love birds, cockatiels, and the small game-like birds that scurried around in the bottom of the cages, Chinese painted quail. He had some sort of relationship with a pet-shop not far away and to which we made frequent visits, and much later when I had a car he would get me to take him to fellow hobbyists for swaps and deliveries. He also introduced me to a rudimentary form of fishing on a nearby canal. All these activities were a million miles away from how I had been brought up, as was the electricity supply, flush toilets and the occasional presence of an Irish lodger who worked in the railway workshops and who brought in some useful income. My vocabulary was broadened by certain of his words that I later realised were an inheritance from his roots in Cumbria. The most memorable was *twerp* which it seems I frequently was.

In his prime, Uncle Leslie had been a main-line train driver with the London Midland Region (LMR) based in Nottingham and on one occasion when being taken to London for a day out, he related not only the gradients and likely speed restrictions along the entire stretch of line but also explained how to calculate the speed of the train by counting the seconds between the quarter-mile posts that he pointed out ran beside the track. 60 seconds times 60 minutes divided by four (for the quarter mile) = 900 divided by the number of seconds that has passed between the two markers. The arithmetic of this appealed to me enormously.

He had for some reason fallen from grace with LMR and it was hinted that this may have been due somehow to my blood uncle, my dad's eldest brother who by this time was getting quite senior with that company. I would never know the truth even though this brother-in-law, my uncle Edmund, was to play a big part in my early post-school life. Certainly there was some needle between the two men. After some intermediary jobs, Uncle Leslie had been re-employed in the industry but at a very different and lower level. First as a blacksmith and then as a painter.

It was during this phase that Aunt Gladys and Uncle Leslie arrived at the farm one day asking my dad to *store* some paint, though if he wanted to use any for the gates, doors, or the house window frames he was welcome to do so. Since however the paint turned out to be all one colour, and a bit "on the bright side" according to my dad, it wasn't ever used and nor was it ever fetched back. Some time later I remember a most indignant Aunt Gladys telling my dad that they had had a visit from the railway police about some missing stock after an anonymous tip-off. It seems that Uncle Leslie had turned his hand to some spare-time external house painting in the neighbourhood. The whistle-blower had apparently noticed that just about all the houses in one street had been painted the same colour. This was a pure coincidence in relation to their storage of the paint as was proved by the accusation not coming to anything.

Aunt Gladys was a great moral supporter of my dad in his difficult early years at the farm and had promised to help financially, if needed, and to come and live there with Uncle Leslie to help run the farm. This offer was never taken up. In any case since she couldn't abide her elder sister who was married to Uncle Harold and since he was already helping by his visits twice a week, the potential for a major family feud did not escape my dad.

Interestingly, he did accept financial help a few years later from his youngest sister Ruth who, out of their father's will, had been privately educated and was by this time a successful schoolteacher. I had been asked in an off-hand manner to ride over to see Aunt Ruth and to pick up a small package that I put casually under the pannier spring of my cycle. On handing the package to my dad, he opened it to reveal what looked like a vast quantity of money notes. I was further involved in several repayment trips over years to come.

Family feuds have one thing in common with national feuds, religious feuds and political feuds: deep historical roots. Fast wind forward fifty years and this youngest sister of my dad is sitting in a lounge chair in a residential home and telling me that when her mother died at a young age, the consensus amongst "those left at home" (that included Aunt Doris – the future wife of Uncle Harold) was to bring back the daughter called Phyllis to run the family house. This duly occurred once Phyllis had worked her notice. But then, Uncle Edmund, the eldest child, stepped in and brought back from her job Aunt

Gladys to run the home. Uncle Edmund of course lived away and so was removed from the fray, but fray it was. Gladys was much more capable than Phyllis and much more noisy and much more bossy. The impasse was only broken by Phyllis having to beg for her old employed job back and leaving the family home for good for a lifetime in service.

And so I have from this old lady of 86 sitting comfortably in her chair, having once again tackled the Telegraph cryptic crossword, and over half a century later, the answer to long-standing family puzzles. The antipathy between Gladys and Doris, the main beneficiary of Edmund's will being Phyllis, the stand-off between Edmund and my dad and finally the reason Gladys braved the rest of the estranged family to attend Edmund's funeral. And all from one small incident arising from sheer bloody-minded cussedness. National wars, religious chasms and political patrician have started from less.

Chapter Four
Secondary Modern

Because of the A, B, & C streaming, Tibshelf school threw up a number of child characters for which my experiences at Newton Junior school, with its bottom-enders and top-enders, had been no preparation. The very fact that the villages were now all mixed up dictated a hybrid of social backgrounds and, it soon became clear, educational standards. Those from the two Junior schools in Tibshelf were way ahead of the rest and conversely those from Hilcote, known as B-Winning because this was the name of the coal-mine, were behind. I decided that those from Blackwell (A-Winning), and Westhouses were about on a par with our lot from Newton. As a result of this, it took the first year for me to catch up with the Tibshelf children. As regards home backgrounds, Tibshelf was a much bigger village and had a spattering of large houses to accommodate professional and business people. By contrast, Hilcote was predominantly a mining community and the children even spoke differently. The pronouns thee and thou were still in use and yet just two miles away in Newton this was not so. Westhouses was a railway village dominated by the main line to Nottingham down the Erewash valley. It had its own railway station and marshalling yards. Blackwell held a mixture of the mining and railway communities.

Colin Churn from Tibshelf came to my attention first. There wasn't much choice in this. At one of the very first morning assemblies when standing right next to me, and without any warning, he fell flat on his face with a frightening bang of his head on the wooden floor. I was dumbfounded and the whole proceedings came to a sudden halt. Once an alarmed chatter had gone round the hall, a teacher rushed in and carried him off. It transpired that he had fainted and periodically from then on continued to do so during assembly and without any apparent harm. Eventually he was excused.

Colin was a quiet and quite brainy boy who after leaving school would become an apprentice electrician. He had a best friend and they were as different as chalk and cheese. In fact he was a stooge to Alan Stapleton the plump joker of huge noise and energy. Alan was very bright and knew it. He had natural repartee and a vast collection of jokes for all occasions. By the third and fourth years, he alone was making advances to girls and one in particular from Hilcote. Elaine was blessed with a fantastic surname, in fact it could hardly have been a better stage name. A stage for us admiring boys to act on. She was Elaine Alcock. What a girl. Good looking, bright and breezy and with attributes way ahead of the rest. She flirted with Alan quite openly in display of her charms. In due course he was to claim success but whether this really was so or just bravado I never could tell. Nor did I ever know if it was he who originated the joke "If you were on a march, would you rather walk up a lane or down a lane. Up a lane if it was Elaine Alcock!"

Alan was an early smoker and also a surprisingly good runner but the main characteristic was his defence of Colin come what may. It was not a good idea to pick on Colin whether or not he was prone to fall flat on his face.

Another boy, whose father had taught him to be an expert coarse fisherman at a very early age, struck a sort of mutually beneficial pact with me. Raymond Hicks might be from Westhouses but his talent did not lie with train spotting but rather artwork. His drawings of coarse fish were extremely good. Through his lectures to me on each fish and how and when it was caught, an idea was born. He could do my drawings and paintwork (with some variations from his own) and I would do his maths. This liaison lasted quite some time and remained undetected. A rudimentary and early form of networking that is, as one will deduce from later life, tantamount to cheating.

Oddly, I developed a friendship with two very different girls. After Mars Bar boy left for a better school, my classwork competitor was another Smith, Jennifer. She was from a very good family in Tibshelf. We often did some studying together and discussed forthcoming tests. She was quiet, well dressed and very pleasant. It's strange but I haven't the faintest idea what happened to her after school and yet, being sort of equals, we should have kept in touch.

Pam Cobb was something else entirely. I very much wanted to keep in touch with her, metaphorically and literally. She appeared on the scene late having been moved to Tibshelf by her parents after living in Kenya. Her father was something to do with the Armed Forces or Government apparently but whatever, she took the elder boys by storm because of her exceptionally good looks and figure. It was the avowed aim to catch a glimpse of her during the brief period of change-over from girls to boys at the swimming baths. Tibshelf school had no swimming facilities of its own so we were taken by bus to Clay Cross to the public baths. Segregation was severe, no mix as in the classrooms but, if the timing was a bit awry, it might happen that the girls were just leaving the pool as we arrived. After Pam appeared on the scene there was only ever one objective on swimming days.

Pam would have remained a distant image of loveliness and excitement had it not been for Mr Finney asking her to assist me in discharging my heavy responsibility as Assistant Editor of the school magazine. To say that I couldn't believe my luck would be a massive understatement and not least because at times nearing publication, we absolutely needed to stay late at school to get everything in. This meant that aside from working in close proximity, I started, as a natural consequence, to walk her home down the village nonchalantly pushing my bike. As time passed I desperately wanted to ask her out for a date but never actually plucked up enough courage. She was way out of my league and anyway I would not have known what to do. This should not have prevented me trying later however, but it did.

As I walked the dogs down our fields and over Dimmie and back through Arthur Ball's cultivated and then rough meadow, it occurred to me that Mr Finney was probably the only teacher actually in the right slot. Maybe there was not much Modern about our school (founded in 1911) but certainly there was much Secondary. Miss Brooks should have been an opera singer, Mr Coupe would pass as a professional bully, Mr Tuschler should be back in Austria brushing up his English (he was the senior English master), the chap that took us for games ought to have retired when he was 85 and Mr Radford would have been better employed just sweeping up my disasters than actually taking Science and Woodwork. To cap it all, the headmaster only ever left his study to take morning assembly.

Whoever invented Secondary Modern school was a genius.. Still, it was a leg up from Newton Primary.

Having a dog, sometimes two at a time, was part and parcel of life on the farm. In the early days it was Darky, a large curly-haired grey male who was a great companion but begot a drama. The drama of a disappearing act. One bonfire night he got out of the buildings and left. We were all very upset. Then, weeks later, my dad saw a tiny announcement in the Derbyshire Times "Dog Found" and the description matched. Off we drove in the tractor to a farm on the far side of Westhouses on the road to Morton. Astonishingly, it was Darky. He had gone miles and were we glad to get him back! But for most of the growing up years we had Bess. She appeared on all the photographs taken with the first box camera and was a magnificent working dog. When I set off to get the cows for milking, even if they were as far away as possible in the top field, the command to Bess to "fetch" would see her bounding down the fields and up the far side to round them up. A wonderful dog was Bess and we always kept her locked in the buildings when she was *on use* since no evil stray dog was going to get at her and give her pups. And how they knew she was always amazed me, but dogs appeared from all directions and would stalk the farm in a wide circle awaiting any chance. An astonishing thing is nature. Bess stayed a virgin. A wonderful dog was Bess.

After a second attempt to keep me at school had failed (this time as a personal letter from the headmaster to my dad which suggested that I sit an entrance exam for the Chesterfield College of Further Education), talk started on what work might be suitable for me when I left Tibshelf Secondary Modern. Since my dad needed some money brought into the house as soon as possible, it became apparent that these expectations centred on my fifteenth birthday and not even staying in the fourth form until the end of the summer term. Apparently I was not likely to learn much more after that anyway.

The point about moving on to Chesterfield College was that it was authorised to set "O" levels whereas Tibshelf school was not. A careers advisor arrived with a bundle of pamphlets that were to be taken home to discuss and "Look carefully at the one called How to Become a Pharmacist". Since I had no idea what a pharmacist did, having never even heard of the word before - in the next village there was a Chemists Shop - I called in as usual on the way home to do the jobs for Great Aunt Pem and as it happened her nephew my Uncle Edmund was there too. They both pored over the pamphlets and when I highlighted the one on becoming a pharmacist Great Aunt Pem expressed vociferously the immediate view that I was certainly not suited to that. They were both taken aback with the imminent prospect of my leaving school. This bright lad who had been given by aunt Madge at age ten The Childrens' Guide to Knowledge because he wouldn't stop asking questions, and by his favourite uncle Harold Thorndykes Junior English Dictionary which had pictures as well as definitions. So it was that uncle Edmund got to work on my behalf.

Following the family tradition of christening the eldest son John, uncle Edmund chose to adopt his rather more posh second Christian name. He started work aged fourteen as a cleaner at the British Rail London Midland Region (LMR) engine sheds at Westhouses. This is not the same as the name infers today. A cleaner (meaning cleaning engines) was the lowest grade in a career that would if successful ultimately lead to being an engine driver.

The job of train engine driver carried great status at that time. The career path was actually from cleaner to passed cleaner (meaning passed out to undertake under supervision the next higher grade of work), then to fireman and to passed fireman and then to engine driver. As I was soon to learn drivers went up, and in their later career often back down, through a grading structure that determined pay and the ability to earn substantial bonuses. The lower grade driver would be shunting freight carriages in sidings, the highest would be driving the main line expresses.

Normally, the pinnacle of a career would be attained by joining the elite Link 1 express drivers. In the case of Uncle Edmund however, he had progressed further by becoming first an Inspector and finally Chief Inspector of LMR based at Leicester station. His responsibilities included passing out the grades and the general operating efficiency of the trains and their crew. It was a very senior position, externally represented by the wearing of a company issue bowler hat.

Sometime after the *leaving school* discussion, Uncle Edmund appeared at the farm and the extent of his efforts to help me was to become clear. His visit was a rare event. There was little mutual respect between him and my dad. At our solitary working sessions down the fields, Dad had once said "your Uncle Edmund will never marry, he's too mean for any woman to have him". But the deep reason was that despite his career success and obvious spare funds, Uncle Edmund had flatly refused to get involved when my dad had really struggled financially and "he'd sooner me have the farm go under than lift a finger to help".

It is certainly true that only Aunt Gladys and Aunt Ruth offered practical support at crucial times. One of my dad's often told stories was that whilst the whole family were still at home, his mother at Sunday tea might say "there is only one egg, that's for Edmund". For his part, Uncle Edmund told me on one of our many future train journeys that "your dad is no business man and never will be". Also, I think he resented the fact that the farm and subsequently the tenanted land had fallen to my dad. In his last years it must have been patently obvious to him that his own cash investments were worth less than my dad's capital as represented by the farm. The twelve years' age gap between the two of them wouldn't have helped either. At that time the head of the family was supposed to command automatic respect irrespective of actions and situations. However, this would have cut no mustard with my dad.

As the years passed, I was to learn that there was much more to Uncle Edmund than his railway career. He was self-educated, widely read and, given a different start in life, ought probably to have been in academia. He was an acknowledged expert on mediaeval England and the reformation period and had given lectures on these subjects in the Leicester area. In his very last years, he was still reading huge tomes on English history while looking after Great Aunt Pem with whom he then lived. Although he worked right through to his 65th birthday, and duly collected his gold watch on retirement, he was to contract sugar diabetes and to neglect himself badly. He died aged 72 a somewhat sad and lonely figure having had a gangrene-infected foot removed at Chesterfield Royal Hospital. He didn't even have time to formalise a gift of £500 he had promised to my mother who, by then, had taken over the most unpleasant role of looking after Great Aunt Pem.

Through his reading and being an organist, he was also very knowledgeable about church and cathedral architecture. A good proportion of his holiday time was spent visiting these places. I never knew from where the music side came but he was the resident organist at Leicester Cathedral for many years and after retirement, at Old Blackwell and then Tibshelf church. He also gave piano lessons conducted from Great Aunt Pem's parlour. The great legacy he left me was a love of walking and generally for the great outdoors and the freedom of remote places.

When I was fourteen, he invited me to join him on holiday. This was to be two weeks at the Holiday Fellowship centre at

Scarborough. These centres were methodist based and therefore alcohol free and devoted to walking the local area. This was a most marvellous experience because everyone joined the A, B, or C groups according to their ability and desire for distance and difficulty. We, of course, were A material because uncle Edmund, as it soon became apparent, was an accomplished rambler and had been on these holidays many times before and indeed to this centre.

I had no walking boots and so the farming boots had to make do, just as they had for football. The procedure was to be taken to the start of a walk by coach and then to follow a leader for a prescribed route. As the week passed, so the walks became gradually longer and tougher. Group B followed the same format with easier walks and Group C basically stuck to the coach. The second big concept was home entertainment. In the evenings at the HF centres, lectures, film slide shows and dances were held. I soon learned the basics of Scottish dancing and such favourites as the Military Two-Step, Gay Gordons and the Valeta. Quite a change from school and farm life.

All these activities built up to the grand concert on Friday night. At this, absolutely everyone with no excuses had to do a turn. Because I had no such turn, it was apparently accepted that I would be part of the play. There seemed to be a selection of well-tried little playlets with well known parts. The lines had to be learned during the week and rehearsed with the other unfortunates that did not have their own slot. I went through the motions with little enthusiasm. The life of a thespian would never be for me.

On the other hand, Uncle Edmund was a revelation. He specialised in monologues. These were lengthy, amusing, known off by heart and always a great hit particularly I noticed with a jolly lady who was here on her own. She started to sit next to him on the coach journeys to and from the walks and they struck up an affable association. The curious thing was that he booked into the centre and insisted on being called John and not Edmund. I heard her ask for his address when we left. On relating this experience to my mum and dad on returning home, they believed that he had had some friendships with ladies met on holidays before and indeed "nearly got engaged once". My dad repeated his staunchly held view that "he is too mean to commit himself to any woman".

Uncle Edmund was never mean to me. This holiday and those of the following two years in Torquay and Hythe were paid for entirely by him. I had no idea what the cost was and had no money of my own. We always travelled by train because through his work he was entitled to a free pass and he knew it would be a novelty for me. This was the time of steam and style. On the outward journey he would sit opposite me puffing his pipe and take out his wallet bulging with paper money. Diligently counting it out, he would proceed to divide the total exactly into two equal amounts. One half went back on one side of the wallet, the other on the other side. "This is for week one and this is for week two". Looking back, what an excellent lesson in budgetary control.

At the end of each daily walk and as we arrived back by coach to the centre, it was my job to jump off the coach first, dash indoors and up the stairs to the largest bathroom, turn on the taps fully and drape our towels on the side of the bath, so reserving the room. Resourceful too, my uncle Edmund. Each Christmas I gave him a two-ounce tin of St Bruno Flake but it was not until he was near to death that I made a meagre payback for his generosity of three wonderful holidays. Holidays that opened up a world of walking moors, marshes and cliff tops, explained the structure and history of Canterbury Cathedral and provided the thrill of riding the Romney, Hythe and Dymchurch steam railway. On his death he left me a specific legacy of £500. All his savings went into a trust fund to pay for the upkeep of a younger sister Phyllis, who for all her life had been somewhat inadequate and not best treated by him.

The purpose of Uncle Edmund's rare visit to the farm was to let us know that there was a vacancy for a junior clerk in the Motive Power Department office of British Railways LMR based at Middle Furlong Road in Nottingham. He could get me an interview because he knew the chief clerk Mr Jennings very well. If I got the job it would open up a career in offices instead of what otherwise would most probably happen, that is, following his footsteps as a cleaner at Westhouses. He was sure that I was much more cut out for an office-based job. My dad agreed and so the die was cast.

The date for the interview was duly set and the programme was to have a medical in the morning at a centre adjacent to the main line Midland Station in Nottingham, go to Aunt Gladys's house for lunch and then to the Motive Power Department for the interview in the afternoon. What surprised me about the medical was the inclusion, and indeed heavy concentration on, an eyesight test. This was no simple "can you read the letters on the third row from the bottom" type check that had been conducted periodically at school. It was all to do with recognising numbers and shapes arrayed in dots of varying colours. Even my acute shyness could not prevent a little query as to why. Apparently I was taking the standard colour blindness test that was compulsory for engine drivers periodically, and indeed the passing of which was mandatory to remain in this elite job due to the absolute dependency on colour signalling. I didn't think there would be a lot of call for signals in the Motive Power office but it seems that "if you want a job on the railways then you take and pass the standard test". So that was that.

What actually happened in the interview proper is totally lost on me due entirely to the drama of being sick half way through. That in turn was due to Aunt Gladys insisting that I ate rice pudding for lunch (or dinner as it was called then) "to build you up for the afternoon". I never could digest milk in its raw state and had been excused it at school since infant days. Whether this resulted from a physiological defect or the sight in my earliest memories of dad milking cows by hand twice a day, I never really knew. The outcome on this crucial occasion was perhaps psychosomatic, perhaps not. At any rate, either through dint of sympathy, achievement or the pulling of strings by Chief Inspector Edmund Smith, I got the job. The start date was fixed at April 9th when I was fifteen years and one day old.

The journey to work involved cycle, train and foot. The archetypal commuter. I had to be out of the door by ten minutes to seven to bike up the lane, down the village bottom end, under the two railway bridges leading to Tibshelf up the treacherous gravel-strewn Station Road and along the *chicken run* to Tibshelf Station, a total distance of about three miles.

This bike ride was great on fine mornings in the summer but horrible in rain and during most of the winter because apart from the bit in the village itself, the route was not made up and the lane in particular was full of potholes and its due share of mud. Cycle clobber including galoshes was essential much of the time. The train left at 7.20 and arrived at 8.00. I never once missed it but only through murderous dashes into the station compound at times. A dash by cycle was somewhat of a forte of mine, after all, had I not been unique in my school for having been pulled up by the local bobby for speeding on a bike when rushing from school on the home run? I have wondered since if prospective police officers have a special time-slot during their training for *The art and execution of sarcasm.* What he actually said was "Are you an alien lad?" As I had no idea what an alien was my blank expression forced an elucidation. "Can you read English? What does that 30mph sign say?" Ah, I pantingly understand, sorry, sorry. Can I go home now, please?

Being thrown together with others in a daily round of what would come to be known as commuting made me aware for the first time of what clothes were being worn. On the farm things were very work-a-day and drab. Overalls, heavy steel-capped boots or Wellington boots, old jumpers and shirts gradually degraded from long-ago Christmas presents and, worst of all, vests. The first time that I didn't wear a vest was akin to any young lady throwing away her corsets.

Here, on Tibshelf station platform, I started to take notice. Inevitably, and along with my friend Terry, there was the girl who had started about the same time as we had. It would seen that the very latest fashion was a form of bell skirt and that the bell was created by metal hoops positioned around the interesting regions of her otherwise slim frame. She held her decorum admirably whilst actually on the platform but whoever had designed this wonder of female attire was obviously oblivious to the need for the young lady to cross to platform 2 each morning. Since this could only be achieved via the open-tread footbridge over the main line, it was as if the whole world was invited to view openly that which was supposed to be covered up. Terry and I tried hard to avert our eyes but it became mesmerically impossible.

As the first summer wore on, so the skirts of this particular girl and of the slightly older girls that boarded the train further down the line, wore off. That is, skirts gave way to long flowing dresses of yellow and red and blue with tight waist bands and super tight tops. Pretty neckerchiefs were worn and sometimes small hats and shoe toes got more pointed and heels got higher. Learning to observe, learning to take note.

For the male travellers, the chilly mornings of April demanded the long raincoat with its wide belt and mandatory trilby hat, or the wrap-around topcoat with its wide lapels or the new-fangled duffle coat with its absurd wooden pegs and rope fastening. Such an outfit might well be complemented by the hard, usually brown, convex shaped hat with its elongated peak. As the weather warmed up, so the thicker garments were dispensed with to leave behind the double-breasted suit, the fancy or not so fancy waistcoat and the stiff white collar. A collar that had been attached to yesterday's shirt using the painful studs at front and back. It was important for the suit sleeve to be sufficiently short to display the cuff links on the shirt and, when the jacket was removed, for the arm bands to glow a brilliant silver colour. Some male commuters had tie pins too. It all added city glamour to the hitherto bucolic experience.

The official designation of *slow* did not relate so much to the actual speed of the train as the fact that it was scheduled to stop at all the stations on the fifteen-mile route. Being steam powered, acceleration from a standing start was sedate and given that stops were made at Kirkby Bentinck, Annesley Central, Hucknall, Bulwell and New Basford before actually passing through a station called Carrington, the journey after the initial novelty was somewhat tortuous. Eventually of course this wonderful little commuter line providing an excellent and economically productive service to the local Nottinghamshire and Derbyshire villages would be scrapped under the Einsteinly-brilliant Beeching Plan. After this act of lawful vandalism the travellers who all worked in Nottingham City would buy cars and make their separate way.

Then, under an equally brilliant plan, a new commuter line would be opened many years later in a (failed) attempt to reduce city congestion from cars and to further the economic prosperity of the East Midlands towns. This new service took a slightly different route cutting out the Derbyshire villages since the original line, that was part of the Great Central Railway terminating at London Marylebone, had been dug up. Of course this destruction had its compensations in that the great gaping hole left by the closure of Nottingham Victoria Station (blasted out of solid rock by the Victorians) was to be filled by the monolithic Victoria Shopping Centre specifically intended to bring hordes of unproductive shoppers into the City as opposed to economic creators.

There might have been more sense in leaving the shops in the villages and then taking the brain-workers into town by developing the well conceived Victorian-created service routes. To compound this fantastical testament to integrated transport and town planning, Nottingham City Centre has now been dug up, at heaven knows what cost and consequential damage to productivity, in order to lay tracks for trams. Less than fifty years ago, there was a good working system of power throughout the city to support virtually silent and electrically driven trolley buses. It is, however, all progress don't you know. Well, if not exactly progress, it all makes work.

It probably took about a year before my intense shyness and lack of contact with real-world adults loosened sufficiently to allow for any sort of conversation with the, by then, regular group of men travelling from Tibshelf to Nottingham every morning. A group of card-players started to shepherd me into their regular compartment. I, the solitary young-man traveller with his wooden carry-case for his lunch and nothing else. A case made especially for the purpose by Uncle Ernie in his joinery workshop in Sherwood Street. Years before he had made a scooter each for me and my sister, the best Christmas present I could ever remember.

What was a man with those skills doing working on a road-sweeping gang? He was the husband of my mum's eldest sister and one of my egg delivery customers. A survivor of the Middle East Campaign in Egypt and then the push from Sicily up Italy to finally rest in Greece, he often told me of his admiration through his war experiences of the Aussies and of his hatred for the Greeks. I never knew why on either count but it seemed particularly cruel that a man who had been through so much ended up with so little leisure. The joinery workshop, the horse betting and the walk down the road to the club for a pint on Saturday night. Once his beloved wife Aunt Annie had died he lost heart and ended up falling onto his own oven top. Poor old Aunt Annie and Uncle Ernie, the only couple to go out with us in the pony and trap when he would catch the horse droppings in a little bucket for his vegetable patch. A lost world.

The train carriages had no corridors. Each compartment was a private little world and the peace of which was disturbed only by the arrival at a station and the prospect, much detested, of someone having the effrontery to open the door and enter. These doors were the slam type that still exist today in certain financially frozen backwaters of the Southern Region of British *Rail* (where did the *Ways* go, perhaps the new name was always intended to focus attention on the stationary hardware and away from the actual moving parts?). The overhead luggage holders were of the string-net type and the pictures were real scenes of sea-side town destinations and set in proper frames, *Visit Torquay for the English Riviera.*

The card game was *nap* and the four travellers played for money. I was incredibly impressed with the system of scoring. The stakes were 1d for 3 tricks, 2d for 4 tricks and 3d for 5 tricks or nap. The keeping tabs was always done by Brian and consisted of pluses and minuses against each named player and written on a pad bought especially for the purpose. It followed that reading across any line of numbers produced zero pence, that is to say it balanced. This was to be a foretaste of dreads to come. It worked such that if for example a winning call was "4 without" thus beating "4 with" when no "5" was called, a win would net the caller 6d and each of the three losers would be reduced by 2d from their cumulative score to date.

Whilst it is often said that in life things even themselves out, this was certainly not so with this little group of gamblers. At a settlement at the end of the Friday evening journey back from Nottingham, it always seemed that Brian was a recipient, that Joe might be if he had had a lucky week but the other two were payers. I often marvelled at this and wondered if there was some deep lesson to be learned since the cards were meticulously shuffled after each hand and, in the course of a week, many such hands were played. It would be great to believe that some blinding insight so detected the cause of these consistent wins by Brian as to ensure for myself a financially successful future by chance. However, this was not to be the case.

I developed a sneaking admiration for Brian due to his laid-back and nonchalant if belligerent air. When not scoring and playing and winning at nap, he completed the Daily Telegraph cryptic crossword with apparently no more effort than it took to read the clues. The only thing I ever knew about him was that he lived on the High Street in Tibshelf, was a civil servant and worked at the Department of Labour situated on the junction of Castle Boulevard and Wilford Road. I knew this because it was on my walking route to Middle Furlong Road and we often walked together.

Joe Wiley was older than the others and was a manager at a motor dealership also on Castle Boulevard. He was extremely kind to me and after about two years would pick me up on Saturday mornings in his Morris Minor and bring me back in the early afternoon. This saved a lot of time because there was no suitably timed train on Saturday and my only option had been to use the Erewash line to Westhouses and this meant not getting home until after three pm.

Working Saturday mornings was a standard part of the week and I so envied Brian and Tom who didn't have to do so in their jobs. Tom was always very smartly dressed and it was through him that I started to wear a top-pocket silk handkerchief, a habit to last a lifetime. He worked for Old's Discount on High Pavement in a position I vaguely thought to be a financial city one although I never understood what he did. He cycled from Morton each morning which was much further from the station than anyone else travelled. During my third year of commuting, he took a holiday in Norway. On his return he talked longingly of the beauty of the Fiords and of the freedom from the rat race. A little later he packed everything in to travel the world and I never saw him again. The fourth member of the card school was a chirpy gum-chewing chap whose name escapes me and I never knew what his job was. Strange how some people make an indelible impression and others do not.

Chapter five
Men of steam

The office that I was about to start work in was attached to the Engine Sheds of the London Midland Region. They were about one mile down line to London from the main Midland Station and across the centre of Nottingham City from Victoria Station. As such it was a long walk that took in, en-route, the third Nottingham station known as London Road that served the east to west traffic. Leaving the office at five-thirty to catch the six ten to arrive back at Tibshelf at seven and home by seven-thirty, made for long days and coupled with the Saturday mornings, made for a long week. Hearing my dad rolling the milk churns up the yard outside my bedroom window early on a Sunday morning gave a first taste of all days merging into one.

The office itself would not be recognised as one today. It consisted of what might be thought of as a church hall with fixed desks attached to all four walls. These desks had steeply sloping lids with a ridge along the top for pens and an inkwell was positioned on the right-hand side. Both pen and ink were still in use. Because the desks were high off the ground so the seating consisted of high padded stools. The only floor mounted conventional desk, located at one end of the room, was huge and accommodated three people; the chief clerk, the assistant chief clerk and a female secretary.

The only private office was situated off this main room and close to where the chief clerk sat. This housed the superintendent. He was the boss of the whole Motive Power Department and was very important. Though rarely seen, he wore a railway issue suit and overcoat and like my uncle Edmund wore a bowler hat. The chief clerk Mr Jennings, who had interviewed me, spent much of each day dashing back and forth into this private office. I never knew why and indeed never knew what either of them actually did.

From the earliest days the role of the assistant chief clerk was obvious. He supervised all of us with a close intensity. He had a specific job of paying the staff each fortnight in cash sealed in a brown paper envelope. My initial fortnightly pay before tax and national insurance was £7-2s-8d. His peculiar sense of humour came into its own on the payday immediately following my successful passing of six months' probation. This event, it seems, triggered my compulsory entry into the Railway Superannuation Scheme and as such, six months' back contributions to the scheme had been deducted from my two weeks' pay. Instead of giving out my pay packet as normal, he felt in his back pocket and handed me three coins. Later he substituted these for a packet containing three shillings. He was a particularly bright man and very good with figures. He had a habit of jerking his head back when walking across the office under time pressure and when thinking hard. His name was Claude Driver and it was rumoured that he had a niece named Betty who was on the stage. This lady became a famous actor and was known to the nation as Betty Turpin in Coronation Street.

The goings-on at or around the top desk was my introduction to office gossip. The secretary to the chief clerk was a fine energetic woman in her prime. She wore loose frocks, had flowing hair and wore the highest of high heels to noisily show off everything to its full potential whilst tripping between the desk, the chief clerk himself and the superintendent's office. She ventured rarely into the vastness of the open office itself. It was said amongst the staff that she enjoyed special privileges from her exalted position and that there must be many secret goings-on because of the intense whispering that went on in this distant corner. Furthermore, it seems she was having a relationship with "a certain member of the general staff, the one that sits down there close to them". As a result, he also enjoyed special privileges by being part of the elite group. Apparently they slipped away at lunchtime together. This outsider was never part of any group staff discussion and his actions had to be viewed with great suspicion. Actually he seemed a pleasant chap and always treated me with great kindness, which just shows that one never can tell.

A new experience for me was the female sounds in a lavatory. Back home, going to the lav. was a solitary affair and even at this time consisted of an earth closet in a separate brick building across the stackyard. Here, however, and although still housed in a separate building across a yard, it was at least a modern-type water flush closet. There was just one lavatory for all the male staff and this was kept permanently locked in order to keep the non-office employees out. The key hung next to the outside door on a string attached to a large wooden block. It followed that if the block was present, the lavatory was free. Otherwise there was no option but to wait and if the occupier happened to be a particular person, this could be a long wait because on certain mornings that person was known to be engaged in the serious business of picking winners ahead of slipping out later to the bookies.

When I first arrived I could have been forgiven for thinking that having plucked up the courage to grasp the elusive key, the lavatory would be as solitary and therefore as private as had been the case at home. It was therefore a massive shock when on about day three, the unmistakable sound of the high heels came clip-clopping ever closer to my little room. With a sound like bedlam a key turned in a lock and a door opened and slammed shut. It was so close it might well have been exactly where I sat. But then the sound as if Daisy (one of our two cart horses) had peed directly onto a concrete floor came as fast as it was noisy. In an instant it was over and the door re-slammed and was locked and the clip-clopping gave away the hasty departure. I was mortified. Only later was I to learn that this event was a standing joke amongst my colleagues. She had a reputation for the most and the fastest in the west. It could be avoided only by the convergence of finding not merely that the male key was available but also that the female in question had gone into the superintendent's room or else was in deep whispering confabulation with the chief clerk. A tricky business.

The cause of the vacancy that I had filled was the promotion of the previous junior clerk to the grade 4 designated post of mileage clerk. Patel, a very polite and well spoken young man whose parents were Indian, had two weeks to teach me the ropes. The main aspect of the junior position was checking in and out the manual work force. This consisted of being handed literally a metal check or disc through my office window flap as men either came on or went off duty. Each check had a number and it was important to put a face and therefore a name to that number so that the time attendance records were accurate and there were no fiddles going on.

The times, counted back to the last minute from the huge clock on the office wall, were entered onto a large weekly sheet against the name of the correct person. This included the mid-day break but not the tea breaks. At first the recognition part was difficult not only because there were hundreds of men involved, but also because some came to the window almost pitch black from their work. A few were pitch black because they were black, the first I had even seen and I formed a view that their race was a far happier one than ours. To a man they always laughed and joked and one in particular always had a banter with me. This was in stark contrast to certain of the others who obviously lived in permanent purgatory.

There was also the smart Alec flashing past the window and throwing in a disc with a speed to match any magician. Eventually though and by compartmentalising the groups by their job titles, it became second nature to recognise the men and to know who had deposited more than one disc in a further attempted slight of hand. Some of the job titles were fascinating. There were, amongst others, Fire Raisers (who built the fires to get the engines into steam), Fire Droppers (who put the fires out and got the boilers ready to be worked upon), Plate Layers, Boilermakers, Shunters and Tappers.

Each day the sheets of the previous working day were extended to produce for each worker the total clock hours taking into account the rules for lateness and leaving early. These figures were transferred to a time card and the sheets and cards passed to a more senior person for checking. By the Tuesday of each week every person in the office had a responsibility for totalling and pricing a batch of time cards. It worked by seniority so that as the sole junior clerk, I would have relatively few cards and only for those workers who tended to have a set week on fairly low rates of pay. The easy pick. There was also one invaluable office aid. Each of the office staff were issued with a company knife that had to be kept razor sharp. This lethal instrument was not intended to damage ones fellow man but rather to scratch out the inevitable arithmetical error. It had no cover for its blade and the shaft was crafted like a straightened-out blade of a turbo prop aeroplane. A truly wonderful instrument that I was eventually to purloin and keep as the finest memento of the years in steam.

On the other hand, the four most senior grade 3 men each had a large batch of cards that included the most complicated employment terms. These complications arose because for the senior footplate men, that is the drivers and firemen whose time details came not from my checking in but from the foremen working next door, the rate for a standard week was pretty much academic. It took a while for me to realise that this work was the real rationale for the existence of the whole office. Footplate men worked round the clock and seven days a week. There was time and a quarter, time and a half, double time and, in the most extreme case of working on a rostered rest day that happened to fall on a Bank Holiday, three-fold time.

In addition to the calculations to produce total clock hours for pay purposes, drivers were paid mileage bonuses. In the case of a daily excursion to a seaside town there was a condition known as short rest under which if the driver spent no more than a given number of hours at the destination, his time was counted as right through from clocking on to clocking off at the depot. Because there were time allowances for the act of clocking itself and for getting from the depot to the mainline station to start work, all this made for a very long clock day. It could for example be from six am to ten pm and since most of these special excursions were on a Sunday, this was all double time. These factors made the basic rate of £11-2s-6d a week for a top driver meaningless in terms of actual earnings and as a result put much pressure on the seniors in the office. (This basic rate made me realise how high were the aspirations of my Aunt Madge when presenting the Children's Guide to Knowledge when I was aged 10 - "one day you will be on £10 per week, mark my words").

So complex were the calculations for the top drivers and firemen and so large the resultant pay that the procedure demanded that every time card once extended into monetary value had to be checked and initialled by a colleague of equal or senior rank. That is why on days building up to payday the assistant chief clerk could often be seen dashing around like a headless chicken grabbing cards fully extended for checking and urging greater speed of extension. When all the cards were complete and priced to gross pay per employee, they were rushed to the pay-office in Derby to be put into Gross to Net Pay terms by machine. The master net pay sheet with individual packets and deduction details per employee was returned on the Friday morning for actual cash payment and with the total actual money pre-calculated into the correct denominations of £5, £1, 10s notes and coinage. Then the fun really started.

Each Friday morning - pay day, three teams of two men each had to be installed in the pay-office that was located in a separate brick building within the main engine sheds. At nine o'clock the security van arrived with the cash, together with the assistant chief clerk who signed for each of the three bags of cash pre-prepared from the three-way split payroll sheets. Each batch of money with the accompanying sheet was handed to the senior in each team for counter-signing. This done, the assistant chief clerk and the security men left, locking we six in the pay-office. Then the race was on. The structure was that two of the teams consisting of senior staff from the office and who were very experienced in the job, took two large payrolls whilst the third team took a smaller payroll. This was deliberate as a form of training for the junior in team three. After two weeks of observation and some practice, I was the junior in team three. It was fortunate that the boss of this team was the recognised fastest and most accurate of everyone and in my case he needed to be. The ability to count out notes and coins was vital but a skill soon learned. The determining quality however was dexterity and here I was found wanting - all fingers and thumbs was an expression that springs to mind.

The procedure was that the first member of each team found the name of the employee on the pay sheet and noted the total net pay. Then to the nearest £5 grabbed such a note from his team's pile of money, next the nearest £1's and so on until the pay was counted out. He then passed the pay packet, that was already embossed with the net pay, name and payroll number of the recipient, to the senior of the team. The second man duplicated the procedure and, if satisfied, stuffed the pay packet making sure the flap was not sealed down.

Since there were hundreds of employees and a decided air of competition in the room, this Friday morning job had a good deal of stress attached to it and this was heightened by two factors. First, there was a noon deadline when the pay-office opened for the collection of wages and secondly if the money did not work out there was no second chance saloon. Money failed to work out if either some was left over at the end or there was not enough to make up the last pay figure. Either was equally serious.

The two senior teams were very slick and always appeared to balance first time and the job would be over by about eleven o'clock. Because the idea was to complete the work just as the pay-office opened for business, these four would disappear once they had finished. I sometimes suspected a bit of trickery, it all seemed too good to be true. This may have been borne out by the occasional excitement directed anytime after noon at Herbert Dale. Herbert was older and more senior than the other staff except for the top desk. He did higher grade work the purpose of which always eluded me except it was something to do with traffic and freight statistics. Not however on a Friday afternoon because he was the official cashier and therefore the payer-out of earnings.

Either instantly on ripping open a packet or very soon afterwards there would sometimes be a rumpus in the works. The person involved and the details very soon penetrated the office, "old Sid is down a quid" or some similar expression would ring out. Herbert had to sort this out but without recourse to those involved in the morning's work since by definition they had not been allowed to leave the pay office until the balance had been struck and therefore everything had been left as perfect. How Herbert did the sorting out was a constant puzzle to me. He was such a quiet cultured man and the outrage of certain workers had to be seen to be believed. I think he must have had some high-level latitude to settle and it was not unknown for "that bloody machine in Derby" to be blamed.

I was never slick. My fingers could not quite build up the speed needed to finish an hour early. The best Roy and I could hope for was to finish about thirty minutes early and, halleluiah, to balance first time. Often though there would be a 10s note left over (or short) and we would have to re-check every packet - which was why they were all left unsealed until the end. I can honestly say that we always found the error eventually and never once did he dig into his personal money or pocket anything. On several occasions we got perilously close to the noon deadline and we might still be sealing packets with the British Railways wet sponge as Herbert approached with his slow steady walk across the yard.

Once when we had had a stupendously successful morning and actually finished just after eleven o'clock, Roy said "as a reward I'll let you into a little secret". Instead of going back to the office he led me through one of the main engine sheds and up the side of the line onto Wilford Road. Having crossed the road we entered a building opposite, went up the stairs and into a huge smoke-filled room. At one of the snooker tables were our four pay-packet-filling colleagues. From that day on, I was accepted as one of the lads.

Just as the terms and conditions attached to the footplate men were structured such that the top few could earn substantially more than the union negotiated basic pay, so the threesome of Ted, Dennis and Phil had managed to work the system to the same end. It took me a long time to discover this and even then only due to the kinship that was to develop between myself and Herbert. It transpired that these three received a higher rate for their work than the official grade 3 due to recognition, albeit on a temporary basis, of increased responsibility. In addition, they were collectively doing the work of four members of the office establishment and to achieve this meant coming in one hour earlier than the official start time each morning and staying one hour later. Also, they worked through their lunch hour break. This constituted higher-grade overtime. Also, when one of the three was on holiday, rather than draft someone else in, the remaining two agreed to cover the work and claim the extra hours. This was an exclusive arrangement to themselves and did not extend to Roy, or the friend of the secretary or indeed anyone else. How it had started and was allowed to continue, I never knew.

Aside from the common work of time sheet compilation and pay packet filling, each member of the office had a very specific job. Ted, for instance, did Sunday rostering. This was an extremely important subject for the more senior footplate men since it was the source of high earnings. To boost the earnings from so-called long days and from high mileage bonuses it was of the essence to work a Sunday because at a minimum it meant double time and should this particular Sunday fall on a rest day, then triple time came into play.

Permutations of choice of driver and fireman for Sunday rostering were endless as Ted explained to me one day. There were two main determinants. One was whether the driver was passed to take a particular route and the second was the system of links. One might think as an ignorant outsider that once the skill of actually driving a steam train had been mastered and especially having undergone the learning curve from being a fireman and then a passed fireman, such trains could be taken anywhere on the rail system. This was not so. A driver had to learn a route and this involved doubling up with an already passed driver and on several occasions building up to being tested on the particular route for real by the likes of my uncle Edmund, the inspection officer. Only on being passed could that driver take charge of a train on a route. Thus this was the first qualifying factor for selection for a lucrative Sunday job. Learning a route involved knowing where all the signals were located, where the gradients and bends were and their magnitude, understanding the station and platform features and most importantly the prevailing speed restrictions.

Every driver once passed had, before every journey, to sign on with a depot foreman and receive that day's printed instructions for the route. These gave all the latest speed restrictions as dictated by engineering works or by any number of special factors. One such factor that always caused mayhem in the foremen's office (that room linked to ours that buzzed with highly charged male activity and choice words) was the passing through the rail network of a royal train since clear passage for the privileged meant disruption to the masses. Information on engineering and other works such as the seismological train or the snow plough train emanated from the central traffic department located in Derby. The dissemination of such routine information and its interpretation into operational instructions was a key job of the more senior staff in our office.

The second qualifier for Sunday working, as with all work allocations, was the *link* into which a driver was placed. Links were the ultimate arbiter of driver selection because they reflected seniority. Only the most senior men were in the top link (link 1). Such drivers would have been in post the longest time, would be passed for the most routes and certainly the main line to London and most vitally would not have failed the crucial and mandatory periodical medical including as it did the colour vision test. Link 1 drivers were the elite and made the most money. At the other end of the scale were link 4 drivers who were reduced to shunting engines around in the marshalling yards or taking freight trains on slow local journeys.

It followed from these two criteria that Ted was often the fulcrum of angry scenes from a driver stamping through the office to his stool demanding restitution for not being allocated a forthcoming juicy Sunday job. Certain drivers got extremely excited and because Ted's desk was towards the centre of the long wall of the office, it was impossible to work whilst explanations were offered. Perhaps it was due to Ted's tall, rather stern and ex-RAF moustached appearance but I never once witnessed a decision being changed or intervention from the top desk. Either he was exceptionally good at his job or else the ultimate authority of his office was always going to prevail. I never knew.

Rest days were another high-earning minefield. A colleague of Ted and sitting next to him was Dennis and one of his jobs was to work out and publish weekly the rest-day roster. He too had his confrontational moments with certain members of the footplate staff. This was because a driver or fireman who was earmarked to work his rest day was in for double money and if that day happened to fall at the weekend or on a bank holiday, then triple time was due. Whilst rest days were quite normal and as such scheduled into the routine matching of men to work, the limitations were severe due to sickness, holidays, absence without leave and the required qualification of being passed for the route and being in the right link. Consequently, and as with Sunday working, a fair deal of judgement went into the choice of crews asked to work on their rest day.

It occurred to me that Dennis was not quite in Ted's league when handling a large and powerfully irate engine driver who had "just been done out of working my rest day". Several times there were red-faced emotional explosions centred on Dennis's area and a small group might gather round to calm things down. Such events presented a baptism of fire for someone as young and innocent as me who had never even heard my parents swear or argue or get particularly emotional about anything to do with work. And here we had two fully-grown men threatening to beat the living daylights out of each other. Of course, much later in my working life there would be confrontations infinitely more deadly if more subtle.

There was a third area of malcontent between the outside workers and a member of our office. We lads were blessed with a second lady member. Lillian was small, a bit on the plump side and, I started to think, not best suited to her specialisation. Lillian was queen of free passes and privilege tickets (P T's). Every employee was entitled to concessionary travel on the railways. The allowance was five free tickets per year and of these three could be, but did not have to be, foreign. Foreign meant outside the region of employment. Working for the London Midland Region therefore entitled the employee, for example, to go up to London five times a year should they choose, absolutely free. Or, say, three times and perhaps to the south coast twice (being partly on the network of a region other than the home region).

Once the free passes had run out, any number of P T's could be obtained and these facilitated much reduced train fares. One would have thought that this valuable fringe benefit would have been a constant source of joy and happiness to all especially since for married employees it covered the whole family. However, this did not prove to be universally the case.

A seemingly endless procession of workers of all types from the most elite driver to the humblest yard labourer sought out Lillian's desk to challenge her records. Herbert with his pay-packets and Ted and Dennis with their Sundays and rest days had their bad confrontational times but at least they were fully fledged men of some senior stature. Poor little Lillian had no such natural armour. Time and again she must have entered the wrong date or the wrong destination because there should always have been one free pass left.

But Lillian's box-card system never lied and there before their very eyes was the evidence in bright blue ink of the passes issued previously. But then, what about the cancellation, what about the late decision to change the destination, what about her errors? Poor Lillian. And when she cried her nearest colleague Arnold would climb down from his high stool and walk over and put his arms round her plump shoulders and tell the offending employee with all the gruffness he could muster to "bugger off". Barbara, the important secretary, would take her out to the ladies to get over it.

I began to wonder if, from the employer perspective, these benefits were really achieving anything. If there was any gratitude from the employee, then I never saw it and if everyone gets the same, can there only be disgruntlement by sort of definition? After all, where is the exceptional advantage? Can there only be the chance of losing out? The chance of being diddled? I resolved to tuck this thought away. It might come in useful later.

During all my three-and-a-half-years in that office, I never discovered what Arnold actually did. What I do remember with great affection was his nickname, which was disparagingly derived from a combination of his squatty frame and his surname of Sidebotham. I also remember his sideline. In this age of smoke and smoking, Arnold was a champion of the briar pipe but the little package that it became my custom to pick up from the specialist smokers' shop on Wheeler Gate did not consist solely of pipe tobacco.

Almost everyone in the office smoked cigarettes and it was common to run out, especially in the afternoon and especially when in urgent need of the key. The closest desk to it belonged to Arnold. The little brown paper package contained an assortment of the most popular brands of fags. Arnold didn't lend out fags or provide a charitable service. He sold them individually and at a considerable mark-up. Everyone knew he was on to a nice little earner but when one needs a fag, one needs a fag and if nothing else his supply never faulted. Arnold was hated but happy. My first encounter with a true entrepreneur.

The only purpose of carrying my wooden case on the pannier of the cycle morning and evening, walking it smartly across Nottingham city and having it under my stool all day, was lunchtime. It contained my sandwiches and nothing else. I was never required to take work home and in fact the concept had not been invented. Solely sandwiches in not wholly true. My mum also packed a pie. Not a steak and kidney pie or a shepherd's pie or anything of that nature but a fruit pie. Whatever fruit was in season on the farm went into a small round tin with a pastry topping. Because she also always packed a small spoon for eating the pie with, I was the subject of some jovial banter in the small canteen area that was next to Arnold's high stool. At first I was hurt by this "mummy's boy" chat but it wore off once it dawned on me that they were all jealous. Never once did I give any pie away

There were a lot of smells in these railway days. Years on and unless one lives in a village lacking mains drains or have plunged suddenly from a clinical aircraft to a Far Eastern city, smells have disappeared. They were very much present in the late 1950's. There is no smoke without fire and no steam without smoke and smoke in an enclosed space such as Victoria Station is smelly. Perhaps it was the frugal practice of making the working shirt last a few days by changing only the collar and only having a bath once per week that made people a bit smelly. Working horses and ponies were plentiful and therefore so were their droppings. All manor of working machinery was not wholly fuel efficient and belching fumes were commonplace. Smog often hung low in the evenings and dampened down the newly discovered chemicals. One was aware of smells.

After about six months I was promoted. It owed nothing to my being the world's or London Midland Region's finest junior clerk. It appeared that Patel was leaving to pursue his career in the retail sector or, more specifically, as he explained to me to work in a shop in the middle of the city that sold wall-paper. As I was to deduce later, this decidedly downward move by Patel was caused partly by the mass of statistical data that had to be memorised to make a reasonable fist of the mileage clerk job, but mainly by the trauma of playing second fiddle to the head of the two-man section.

My first real clerical position placed me at the bottom of the grade 4 salary scale and represented quite an increase in pay. I was over the moon with the letter from the chief clerk announcing my new status and terms but it did not seem to impress my dad greatly. Still, mum increased my pocket money.

The mileage section turned out to be all to do with the determination of bonuses earned by the footplate staff. Mileage bonus was staged according to the total mileage covered in each week. Not that my new position involved the actual calculation of money but just the mileages. As with the hours aspect of pay, details per man were fed to the offices in Derby for conversion into money and the subsequent payroll. The routine was quaint. In the adjoining foreman's office was a sliding window through which was pushed the daily journey sheet of each driver and fireman after it had been approved with the initials of the foreman on duty at the end of each shift.

On our side of the wall was a large wooden box into which these sheets dropped. As a result, this box was about half full each morning and positively packed on a Monday morning. The task was to convert the journeys into mileages and tot up each stage to give the shift total. There was no difference between the work of the junior and senior positions aside from the quantity of sheets that could be processed. This in turn depended upon knowledge and memory and the ability to graft. In essence it was no different to a factory production line with the speed of the belt self-determined by these factors.

The fact was that a new hand had no knowledge. Mileages from one point to another had to be looked up on a series of cards that had been written out over the years by previous incumbents of the position. The longer this research took, the slower the processing and the larger the pile of un-cleared sheets. The same deadline as applied to time for payroll input applied to mileages. Missed input to Derby would inevitably lead to held-over bonuses and when this had occurred in the past, angry drivers had stormed in seeking the blood of the mileage section.

Whilst it would take time for me to learn the journey mileages, there was a limit to how long I could be carried on the section. As far as Patel was concerned, the limit had been passed and colonel John Redmond had been forced to recommend a change. The colonel was a fairly fearsome and self-contained character. Short, bald and with heavy rimmed spectacles, he did not mix with the others and chose to keep himself to himself. He had no truck with the office gossip and did his job diligently and efficiently. His good army pension added to his independence. Also, he was the only one in the entire office who came to work by car.

Being terrified of failing and not having met anyone remotely like my new boss before, there was no way the colonel would be displeased with my work effort. My head was down over those sheets and the mileage cards from the minute I got there until I left. The effect of this was probably exaggerated by the fact that the colonel was doing no overtime or covering other positions or higher-grade work and so did the bare minimum hours. In fact rather less. He walked in just a little late and usually left just a little early.

My endeavour, coupled to a good memory for numbers, paid off. Less and less was there a need to refer to him for route details from the start to the finish of a journey and more and more I learned the routes common to each link. Soon, only the complicated Sunday specials presented any problem and I soon discovered that they did for the colonel too. So it was that we started to get on well together and to the point that sometimes by mid-afternoon we engaged in a little game. Once we were straight up (no sheets waiting to be done) we would open our side of the box and take turns to surprise the next unsuspecting pusher-through of his sheet by whipping it out of his hand from the tip first exposed to us. We would then revel or groan depending on the simplicity or complexity of the sheet thus obtained.

I must have pleased the colonel really because he started to take me in his car across Nottingham to my station after work on his way home. It was on these journeys in his Ford Popular that I learned just how awful every other single driver was and how proficient he was. It must have come from his army training but the anger and invective from inside that little car had to be seen and heard to be believed.

Actually, the train journey mileages and routes were interesting in themselves. I began to like my job. The crack train in the week from Nottingham to London St Pancras left on time every morning at precisely 8.04 am and took two hours and four minutes. This was the prestige route and allocated to only a link 1 crew. It ran via Leicester round the

Trent loop (where the trains from Derby joined the track) and had a total mileage of 127. This consisted of 28 to Leicester, and in 28 minutes, and 99 forward to London. Unlike today however, this was not the sole route to London. Trains were scheduled via Melton Mowbray also, on track long since abandoned apart from local journey specials on cute little steam trains run especially by the enthusiasts for the tourist. This route to London via Melton was, at 123 miles, that bit shorter.

At the other end of the spectrum were the many freight trains especially carrying coal. The places themselves were unknown to me except as specific mileages between each and in total. There is a touch of irony in that many of these places would become known to me intimately years later, whilst the mining industry being served would be wholly eradicated. Go north east to Calverton, Farnsfield and Bilsthorpe or north west to Hucknall, Linby and Papplewick. These coal pits fuelled the power stations located on the banks of the rivers Trent and Soar that in turn fed the east midlands with electricity and served the national grid. But it would take a job move to appreciate this.

I started to appreciate the steam engines that hauled these great loads and sometimes when the colonel and I were straight up I wandered through the massive motive power sheds to get close to these fantastic examples of British engineering. I loved the little 0-4-2 and 4-2-2's and started to identify for myself the engine that pulled the trains along the track just one field away from our top field on the farm. This was the little branch line taking coal from the pits at Teversal and Pleasley down to the main Erewash valley line at its junction at Westhouses and on to who knows where. Down was the operative word because rail track is supposed to be as near flat as possible and hence the steep embankments, tunnels and viaducts. The constructors of this branch line either forgot this or more likely decided its worth was so little as not to justify the effort. Consequently, when the full load reached a point opposite our field, the crew had to stop the train, alight and walk from wagon to wagon applying a brake to each by hand. There was still a driver, a fireman and a guardsman but their leisurely stroll along the length of the train and the overall journey time schedule was a million miles removed from the 8.04 to St Pancras. It taught me a powerful lesson for the future. Never reckon that people with the same job title or professional label, even having an identical start to their career, are the same. The top of link 1 and the bottom of link 4 exist everywhere.

If the little engines were lovable, the giant 8 and 9 freights were positively awesome. Their magnificence was not dented by the quietness and stillness of being at rest in the great engine sheds. Nor was their dignity impugned by the ant-like men in boiler suits with strange sounding trade names who crawled over and inside them. Years later when the last working beasts in the UK had long since taken a dead-end journey to the breakers yard, I was literally reduced to tears when my taxi entering Cochin in Southern India came to a shuddering stop to allow an 8 freight to pass over the level crossing hauling its gargantuan load of coal. What the British introduced, the ex-colonials had had the sense to retain.

Of all the staff in the office, two stick in my memory most. Ted because of the lunch-time horse-play when he was to demonstrate to the others, and on me, some of his RAF close-combat fighting skills. He had some technique, was much taller than me and had secured a strange sort of grip but he was a chain-smoker and perhaps unaware that I had mucked-out the cows for years and was used to heaving sacks of corn and potatoes. Anyway, I only hit him once in the lower lumbar region. He sank slowly to the floor and rested. Ted did not do his overtime that day and in fact left slightly early. He was off for six weeks.

The other was Herbert because he reminded me of Uncle Harold with his quiet authoritative manner and because in the afternoons, not Fridays, he had the ability to go soundly to sleep whilst sitting bolt upright at his desk over the statistical returns that I never understood. But more importantly because one afternoon overlaying his vital returns I spotted a diary. Not the main body holding the days, but the rear section containing complex grids with zigzag lines in blue ink. To most they would remain a mystery and in the office were no doubt thought of as useful references for his scientific work. To me however they were recognised instantly as diagrammatical representations of bell-ringing methods.

Some months before and having cycled to Matlock on a Sunday afternoon with my best friend John Smithson (who was 10 days younger than me and for who's mother I had often been told nurse Ball had had to leave my mother to attend in a snowy April of 1942), there was panic to get back fast. It seemed he had to be at Old Blackwell church by a quarter to six to ring the bells. This was news to me but apparently for the past few weeks he had been receiving lessons from his dad and was in the team ringing the treble.

We walked not into the main entrance of St Werburgh's church but in the side door to the vestry, turned sharp left and having opened a small wooden door climbed the circular stone steps until opposite was a door with a handle at its foot. The technique was to step onto the opposite stone ledge and pull up the door and whilst holding it aloft, step inside. The room inside was a revelation to me and I entered a new world. There were five men with coats off and sleeves rolled up and six ropes with a thick brightly coloured middle section draped round pegs in a circle but climbing up through their own little hole cut neatly in the ceiling. This was the holy grail, the bell-ringing chamber, and we were late.

John took off his coat, rolled up his sleeves and walked sheepishly to the bell rope on the far side of the chamber. The rope was untied from its peg and its end held in the left hand along with a few loops of loose rope. The right hand held the woollen middle section. Slowly the chatter stopped and five men did the same with their appointed bell rope. I cowered in the background and watched. John tugged the centre section of his rope downwards and the others followed in rotation in a clockwise direction. Immediately the bells started to clang, 1,2,3,4,5,6 from the highest to the lowest note and repeat and repeat. After each round the middle woolly section moved higher and higher until almost touching the ceiling with all the spare rope taken up. After a few rounds of this extreme length, John's dad shouted "stand next sally" and from 1 to 6 the middle section or sally was slowly eased to rest where it had started.

Awestruck was not in it. Mesmerised would be a better description of how I felt. That Sunday evening's session was not the best advertisement for the art of change-bell-ringing. John had not yet got full control of the bell or the striking art of the treble. There were numerous clashes of bells and consequential yells from Arthur, John's dad and bell-ringing captain, attempting to get others back into the correct sequence. Rather than putting me off, this cauldron of human effort somehow drew me in. It looked physically and mentally hard and when Arthur asked if I would like to see the actual bells before the next mid-week practice, the die was cast.

Blackwell church has six bells with the largest, the tenor, weighing 7cwts,2qrs and having a diameter of thirty-four and a half inches and tuned to note A. It is believed that originally the tower had just three bells and the second bears the mark of the Nottingham founder Henry Oldfield with the legend *Jesus be our Spede, 1587*. These facts are set out in an excellent little book written and compiled by Glyn Holdgate and published in 1999 *Ting Tangs, Trebles and Tenors*. It records that in 1901 two further bells were added as cast by John Taylor at the

Loughborough foundry and that of the reconstituted five bells, the Oldfield bell became the fifth.

Although completely ignorant of this history at the time, this fifth bell was to become mine for a five-year period until 1964. The first full peal on the five bells was achieved in 1928. In that same year, two young men who would become very special to Blackwell church rang their first peal on these bells. One was the Arthur now inviting me to "take a look at the bells" and the other was Wilf Riley who quite co-incidentally was my dad's nearest neighbour. Wilf and his family lived in a bungalow in an adjoining field across from our *back field* and from where, apart from his full-time job in the coal mine, he ran a small but flourishing market garden business. He was the proud owner of a Javelin motor car the likes of which I had never seen before and have never seen since. These same two men also rang a peal to celebrate a lifetime as bell-ringers. It was achieved on the fiftieth anniversary of their first peal. A truly fantastic feat.

One of the very last peals to be rung at St Werburgh's, Old Blackwell on the five bells before the augmentation to a full six, took place on 15th August 1945 and was one of only a handful of peals of the full 5,040 changes in the country to take place actually on V.J.Day to celebrate victory in the Far East and the end of hostilities. Of the team that day, three were present and still actually ringing as I watched fourteen years later. Each man proved to be quite remarkable and collectively they taught me one very important lesson that would stand me in good stead throughout my later career. Never underestimate the mental capacity of a seemingly humble person. Absence of opportunity and even ambition is no guide to ability.

Arthur had been elected tower captain at the age of 21. He had lost half of his right arm in an accident towards the end of the war. He was a shunter of freight wagons in the railway sidings at Westhouses both before and after this accident. He re-mastered the art of bell-ringing using his good arm and hand and the stump of his amputated arm. He also looked after the tower, tended to the bells, repaired the stays and wound up the clock for a total period of 55 years.

If ever there was a true Knight of the Realm, it was Arthur Smithson. The second longevity medal should have gone to Albert Wheeler who rang the tenor and heaviest bell. Back in 1945 he was undertaking his first peal in that valedictory ring and was the backbone strong man. He was a train driver and in my first year of work a solid respect for this skill had been growing. He was an excellent ringer and his striking skill on the tenor was such that he was an obvious challenger to Arthur who, because of his handicap, could only operate on the No2 or No3 bell.

However, despite some needle between the two men, he was never a serious contender for tower captain because Arthur's rope sight was far superior. Albert was a widower and drove to church in a Baby Austin car often accompanied by a lady friend who was later to become his second wife. He was a dedicated pipe smoker and in an era when whether it was safe to fake (draw into the lungs) cigarette smoke was already being debated, Albert took deep lung draughts of pipe smoke that made his eyes almost pop from his head. Not that that did any apparent harm. He was over 90 when he died.

The third man was not Harry Lime but Billy Steele. It had not been Billy's first peal in 1945 and he remained a faithful member of what was to become a very sophisticated and technically proficient team. He came from solid farming stock was small in stature and always immaculately dressed in collar and tie. A true gentleman in the old fashioned sense and marvellous to get to know and to talk to.

Flashing down Cragg Lane on my bike the following Wednesday evening having barely had time to gulp down my meal after cycling from the train station, I passed Arthur peddling his old sit-up-and-beg model and slowed down to ride together to the lich gate. He led the way up the stone steps of the tower but passed the door to the ringing chamber until after a further revolution we stepped onto a ledge and through a door into a small room the principal feature of which was a large glass case. Arthur opened the case with his key and from a ledge pulled out a large handle and inserted it into its housing.

Without a word he started his twice-weekly job of winding up the church clock. For a one-handed man this was no mean accomplishment since the mechanism was heavy and the drop deep. I was innocently amazed. It had never occurred to me that church clocks had to be hand-wound. That this was happening as an act of casual routine by such a disabled man, and had been for many years without help, created a sense of immediate admiration. It proved however to be small fry compared to what would follow. Having re-locked the mechanism we left the clock chamber and walked higher up the stone steps that led to the bells themselves. Their size seen at this close proximity was huge as they hung dormant each in its wooden cage lined up in two rows of three and here began my first lesson.

Arthur took me round the bells on a wooden catwalk pointing out the smallest treble and graduating to the largest,

the tenor. He explained that attached to the wheel-like frame of
each bell, and now in an upward facing position, was the stay
and that when the bell was fully inverted and so upside-down,
this stay could travel a few degrees off the perpendicular
before hitting against a cross beam designed to stop the bell
traversing completely. It was a safety device for someone such
as he hoped I would become, namely a learner. A skilled bell-
ringer could hold a bell in the upside-down position just off
centre and with minimum physical strength awaiting the
precise split-second to pull-off and strike at exactly the right
time in relation to that bell's correct position in a sequence of
changes. Such a sequence of changes was known as a method.
There were simple symmetrical methods and surprise non-
symmetrical methods.

The true skill was the timing of the strike and a big bell
would take longer from pull-off to strike than a smaller one.
Thus it may be that the tenor would pull off before the treble
and yet strike later. The skill of holding the bell balance whilst
upside-down largely negated the need for physical strength
once the bells had been rung-up. This was important because it
meant that females could become expert bell-ringers and
indeed some of the best ringers that Arthur had tutored had
been girls. My head was swimming with facts but this one I
was more careful than the others to tuck away for future
reference.

This first teach-in was concluded by the classical
prospective bell-ringers' dire warning. Before the necessary
skill of rope handling was attained, the bell in its dangerous
upside-down position might fail to be held just past
perpendicular and if so, the sheer weight of the bell could so
smash the stay against its cross beam (the slide) as to break it.
If this happened, the bell would do a complete revolution and
the bell-rope that traversed it would rush to the ceiling of the
ringing tower. If the unfortunate learner was still hanging onto
the rope, it followed that a swift upward journey was enforced
and it was not unknown, as was the case at Blackwell, for the
ceiling to intervene. The same accident would occur if during
normal ringing the sally failed to be caught in order to hold the

balance. This possibility haunted me throughout the bell-ringing years and led to several sweaty nightmares.

And so it was that my bell-ringing career started. First the handling of the bell. In one-to-one little sessions before mid-week practice nights Arthur patiently taught me how to ease the bell from its resting position into gradual first movements to-and-fro by slight downward pulls on the sally and gradually increase the momentum until this brightly coloured blob of wool was almost touching the ceiling on its upward flight. The crucial bit was to catch the sally as it returned lest, once in full flow, the bell should rush over the top. If this happened, the rope would take me with it to the ceiling. It is a truly wonderful feeling when the fear goes and the bell can be held just past its balance in the inverted position. This keen learner could handle a bell.

Next came ringing up with the team on a light inside bell. The skill is to follow precisely the bell in front by facing that bell-ringer and pulling the rope just after his and if going too fast then to slow down and vice-versa. It takes time to master this task and even more to ring down at the end of a session since once the bell is in free-flow and off the balance, there is little or no control and yet the follow-my-leader must be maintained for the sound of the bells to be rhythmical and musical. Once these rudimentary operations become easy, the true skill is accurate striking. This means timing the hit of the clanger on the face of the bell such that the resultant sound is evenly spaced with the other bells. When a team of ringers are striking together well, then the sound is lyrical and melodious. Conversely, if the spacing of sound is uneven, or worst of all clashing, then the noise is dreadful. A bit like getting life right or wrong.

Perfect striking calls for highly skilled rope handling and a good ear. It soon became apparent that some quite adequate ringers never made good strikers. There was more required than conscious observation. Sub-conscious timing was of the essence. Big takes longer, small takes shorter. Two valuable lessons that were to be tucked away and applied elsewhere, but much later. After the technique comes the application.

The art of change-ringing is about methods and methods are about extracting a given number of bell combinations without duplication and without returning to the 1 to 6 (or less or more) strict sequence. In its extreme, 5,040 (6x5x4x3x2x1x7) changes are mathematically possible on six bells provided the rotations are consciously changed to set patterns. Such a feat is called a peal and would take typically two and three-quarter hours to complete. For the whole of this time concentration is intense and even with six experienced competent ringers familiar with the chosen method, mistakes are almost certain to be made. This is where the most skilful factor of all comes into play, rope sight. A few highly gifted individuals, and Arthur Smithson was the most gifted that I ever knew, could from one ringing position and whilst ringing a method themselves, correct errors made by others and sometimes by several others simultaneously.

Because a method involves exact rules of where to interchange sequence positions with another bell (dodging) and where to stay in a position (holding), it follows that to keep right on one's own bell for long periods is very difficult. To do so and correct others at the same time is nothing short of miraculous. It was something that I could not master. But then, a one-armed man dedicated to a church bell-ringing team and bringing on new learners for fifty-five years, winding up a heavy clock mechanism, keeping the grounds tidy, riding a bike, doing a full-time job, setting a vegetable garden and bricklaying for a local farm, is a miracle.

I was a keen student and learned so much from this marvellous man. Three things always stayed with me. Never be content to stick with what has been learned so far, there is so much more. Proof; I graduated from simple Bob Minor as a method to what was generally accepted as the most difficult of all, London Surprise and developed from just ringing to conducting and achieved a number of peals with this excellent team. Next, and whether it is corny or not, there is no more powerful organism in this world for achievement than a small closely knit team of like-minded people all pulling together and lastly, and most important of all, it is possible to look straight ahead and yet see what is going on to one's left and right.

The journal The Ringing World has been published weekly since 1911. In it was advertised their official diary. In this diary I had been studying the various bell-ringing methods on the increasingly tedious morning train journeys to Nottingham. The path of a bell throughout a method was drawn as a diagram across pages until the whole sequence was covered. In addition, the rules at the conductor's call of "bob" or "single" to change the routine, were shown separately.

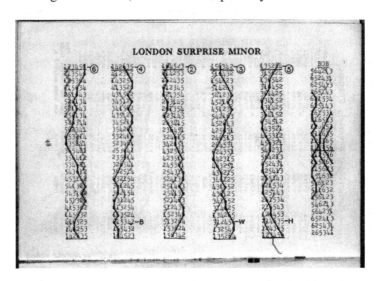

There are simple methods like Bob Minor, Double Bob and Grandsire and more complex surprise methods such as Oxford, Cambridge, Kent and the dreaded London. To see Herbert doing the same concentrated work in the motive power office was like finding a long-lost friend. After I had tentatively expressed my interest, it was as if we two were drawn into some secret society. I had unwittingly penetrated a part of Herbert's secret afternoon armoury. Soon we were deep in discussion about some of the more tricky sections of the surprise methods and before long I was being invited to the practice evenings at the two big city-centre churches. I was way out of my depth at both.

St Peters was dominated by undergraduates from Nottingham University and although occasionally getting a ring, my time was spent mostly marvelling at eight bells rung to complex pieces and a hotbed of animated discussion. These Thursday evenings were alternated with Mondays at the absolutely huge St Marys church in the Hockley district. This was a quantum leap from Blackwell having all ten bells regularly in use and seeing two men standing on a box handling the two-ton tenor. How I envied the student bonhomie and the city's night time energy. How I enjoyed the half-pint after work with Herbert and picking up his habit of a mini pork-pie from under its glass cover with mustard and a knife. The cost of this extra-work activity was increasing tiredness. No sooner had I got to bed after catching the last train back, than I seemed to be getting up again.

The feeling of great tiredness and the difficulty in getting up on Sunday morning to ring for morning service (my one day off) was not being helped by a recent decision to attend Clarendon College on two nights a week for a course on shorthand, typing and English. The mileage clerk's job was now boring and there was no prospect of moving to one of the other sections since the little deals to cover higher grade work and absences with overtime stifled any openings, or so it was beginning to appear to me. Another thing was that mysterious punch cards from the Hollerith section in Derby were starting to replace some of the manual work in the office. There were vague rumblings about computer analysis and the future being in Derby not Nottingham. There were vacancies being advertised internally for jobs at the Derby offices but to get there I would need a motorbike that I could not afford. Being turned down for an *outward bound* course sponsored by the Traffic Department in Derby did not bode well either.

As by now an avid reader of the evening paper on the train home, the answer was to become a journalist and for that shorthand was needed and hence the course. The English part was interesting and ought to be kept up. The touch-typing came easily and I passed a 30-words-a-minute exam at the end of the first term but the key shorthand part was not working. What was the point of learning the Pitman swish curve only for it to be replaced the following week? My ambition to become a journalist was receding. There was a man often on the later trains with thick-rimmed spectacles and bulging eyes who kept wanting to touch me and had some good suits at home that would fit me and I should visit him at the weekend and try them on. It was time to move on.

Chapter Six
Finance is calling

After the extreme shyness amongst girls at school and the egregious attempts to date the one special one on the school magazine, my early attempts to have any semblance of a girlfriend were both bumbling and cautious. Cautious probably because, and certainly influenced by, my elder sister. She was hot and wild and out and about in the tight slit skirts and high heels that were all the rage in the early 1960's. She was out of control and a big and constant worry to mum and dad. She would not stay in and she would not dress decently. Even if I had the time to, or was it opportunity, I was not going to add to their worries. That is, I wasn't until Betty came along. There had been girls before. I had taken Glenys from the railway office to the ABC cinema in Nottingham several times and I really, really liked Linda whom I met on the train with her pretty printed dress, laughing eyes and sheer excitement. The Saturday afternoon help on the farm for my dad was even sacrificed for Linda as I set off by bus for Chesterfield and then a second bus to Newbold to meet her parents and take her to the pictures in Chesterfield. We saw Pat Boone in April Love and held hands and snogged. But no further.

My friend David Cantrill had recently started to learn bell-ringing. He was tall, fair and good looking and one Sunday evening at church introduced me to Sandy "a friend of my new girlfriend". These two girls came from Sutton-in-Ashfield where he had met them. A foursome was arranged at Sandy's house on a cheerful little street in Sutton to listen to some music on her record player. This was repeated several times when her parents were out and somehow we two couples got separated in the two small downstairs rooms so David could spend some time alone with his girlfriend. Sandy was warm and cuddly and much more experienced than me but the furtive circumstances and the sickly overpowering perfume just put me off. I stopped going.

Then it just happened. Like a bolt from the blue. Arriving early for bell-ringing on a Sunday evening I was met at the belfry door by this tall, leggy, blonde with the most beautiful face I had ever seen. She had finished with David and wanted to be my girlfriend. To her I looked like Paul Anka and ever since she first saw me she couldn't stop thinking about me and she wanted to be with me from now on and for ever.

It was as if the world's greatest illusionist had stepped onto the stage and spirited away the box labelled shyness, the jar labelled caution and all other girls in their pretty dresses too. I just knew instinctively that this was it. My pulse was racing, my heart was thumping away and as I reached for her hand she came straight to me and we hugged in silence. Enter Betty and my world turned upside down.

It was just unbelievable. This ravishing girl who could have stepped off the front page of any fashion magazine and have her portrait as the enlarged centre-piece of any photographer's window display, wanted to be with inconsequential me. Me, the railway clerk, the farm labourer, the rural bell-ringer. The no-hoper with girls. She had no inhibitions. I had no inhibitions. This ugly duckling turned swan. The all-in-one once-and-for-all-time confidence booster. We could not keep our hands off each other. Her face vividly flushed, her whole body shaking, she would pleadingly urge me "not to do anything silly". Me, (whose sister was running amok and who would shortly become pregnant by a sixteen-year-old apprentice builder) who was now being given a stern talking to by my dad after he saw us going into one of the farm buildings and ending with "she is only fourteen you know". We did try to cool it and we did pledge to wait until we were older. But how much older?

The big difficulty we had, and maybe a blessing, was how to meet. We were totally reliant on buses to bridge the five miles or so distance between us. As a further obstacle, her parents were not to know of the relationship and indeed I never met them. All I did know was where she lived and that she was adopted and did not know her natural parents. This probably explained their refusal to let her meet any boys but this would never have stopped Betty. She was a master at subterfuge and had girlfriends to visit and churches to go to.

We met mostly on Sundays, my heavenly day since that first time, but she would appear as a surprise sometimes in the week and be waiting near the bus stop for when I rode past on my way home from the railway station. Best of all, she would get a secret message to me that she could board my train at Kirkby Bentinck station and travel with me the one stop to Tibshelf. She would have to have caught a bus to get there from where she lived and would be holding her pet poodle.

When this first happened it caused a sensation with my fellow travellers. This beautiful tall young lady with her poodle getting on to travel with Smithy and then walking with his bike back to the farm. Word got back to the office where I was counselled in one quarter to be "very, very careful" and advised in another quarter to "go for it or you'll regret it". Betty had no money at all apart from pocket money but somehow she managed to buy me some wonderfully touching presents that I treasured for many years. A silver coloured cigarette case, a yellow cravat, several sets of cuff-links and her heartfelt 45 record, Acker Bilk and his Paramount Jazzband playing *I got my love to keep me warm*. Each time I took her to the end of her avenue to meet the curfew, the ache would start and it continued until we met again. There would never be anyone else. But there was.

She was a red-head, very bubbly, bright and laughed a lot and somehow different from the others. I asked her for a date and we went to see Charlton Heston in Ben Hur. We were both in some sort of transcendental whirl and went for a walk afterwards down towards the Nottingham arboretum. We held hands and it was incredibly exciting. We agreed to continue seeing each other and I told her about Betty and said I would end the relationship.

I met Betty in Mansfield Market Place at lunchtime and told her there was someone else and perhaps we had had to wait too long and perhaps there were too many obstacles. She cried and cried and slowly walked away with her beautiful head on her elegant long neck bowed. I never saw her again and even though I have had the love of two good women since, there will always be regrets about time and about life and what-ifs. I had just finished reading a book by Connie Clausey titled *I love you honey, but the season's over*. It concerned a circus leaving town. God forgive me. Surely she would have met a man who would give her a far better life than I ever could?

Years later I returned to the office in Nottingham after lunch and a colleague said there had been a telephone call for me from a woman who had seen me in the car and who did not leave her number but would ring back. I waited but she never did. It would have been Betty.

The small jobs ad. read "Junior Clerk wanted East Midlands Electricity Board, Lime Tree Place, Mansfield". The salary was quoted as £330 a year and, although £20 a year less than my present pay, and although surely I was two-and-a-half years on from being a junior clerk, I began to weigh things up on the journey home. No hours and hours spent on the trek to Nottingham six days a week. I could cycle to Mansfield and I reckoned that although hilly, the service bus could probably be beaten and so that meant a journey time of about 30 minutes or less. It would be cheap and I would save the whole of the rail fare and, furthermore, I liked the sound of Lime Tree Place. What a fantastic sounding work location. A world away from Middle Furlong Road and the rows and rows of back-to-back cheap tired houses and the outside lavatory with its noises.

And another thing, although I loved the railways and had great respect for the men who spent a whole lifetime working on them, it would be a relief to be rid of the ever-present stigma attached and the passionate unescapable need I always felt to defend the system. "Look", I would say, "You cannot compare the price of rail travel with road. The railways maintain their own track and signals and have a self-contained independent network. How can that be compared in cost terms with just getting onto a ready-made road and driving away? What about maintenance, what about signs?" But I always ended up as a minority of one, overwrought and frustrated and of course the Beeching Plan would come along and prove the uneconomic case for much of the local network of railways. My own commuter line would be ripped out along with hundreds of other local service lines. The claimed financial benefit to future generations would be enormous. So it was good to turn away; the alternative was probably to explode, as I still feel like doing when I think about it today.

There could surely be little to defend in the shiny new electricity industry. Overall, the attraction was overwhelming. Still, I was getting paid well now especially with the overtime through working bank holidays that I always volunteered for and the free passes (especially to London) that had become increasingly attractive. I turned the idea over in my mind until Saturday afternoon and then went into the cowhouse where my dad was milking to get his seal of approval. "Please yourself John, they're both nationalised industries so you won't have to work hard in either". Hardly the glowing encouragement I was craving but as usual he had a point. It seemed big and safe and I did like the idea of Lime Tree Place.

The interview was at the Lime Tree Place office block, which turned out to be a large, ugly, utilitarian brick and concrete building next to the Gas Board offices and close to the sprawling Mansfield Brewery site. It was conducted by a Don Smith who was introduced as the head of administration at this the Mansfield and North Nottinghamshire District, and Harold Lucas head of the Income Section within which the vacancy apparently lay. Both were very pleasant men and treated me gently and kindly.

After my smooth passage for the railway job in Nottingham, I began to think that I must have a natural talent for interviews especially since most of the time was spent with me explaining the finer points of bell-ringing. This held the senior man in obvious rapt attention. There was no doubt in my mind, as the discussion wound to a leisurely close, that I would be offered this most junior of jobs and especially after I had mentioned that my dad had had to pay a *capital contribution* towards the cost of getting an electricity supply to the farm some two years earlier. I consciously held back the information that he had refused permission for the Board's Wayleave Officer to enter the land to inspect the overhead lines on the grounds that it was a ploy to get sightings for "more bloody poles". Of course this was no personal affront to the unsuspecting wayleave man, my dad just hated all officials of any kind, and in any case, the wayleave payments were a pittance far outweighed by the trouble of working round the poles and their bracing supports.

Many years later, my wife's best friend Diana died a long slow death from cancer and along the way I became friendly with Diana's husband who rose to be Chairman of this same Electricity Board. He told me a story about how, as a young thrusting engineer in a rural district, he had been asked to go and see a retired senior military man (second in command of the Berlin airlift at the end of the war) to persuade him not to object to plans to erect an overhead line on fields in the view from his large imposing house. After giving John coffee and sitting him down in a comfortable armchair, the distinguished war hero sat opposite and said very gently "look Mr Harris I came to live here for five negative reasons, no road traffic, no aircraft noise, no neighbours, no tourists and NO BLOODY ELECTRICITY POLES". The overhead line went up anyway.

As I was getting up to leave, Don Smith said he would like to set me on but there was a snag. A snag? This vacancy was expected to be a route to better things and the successful candidate would be enrolled on a day release Business Administration course at the local West Notts Technical College. The snag was that the minimum entry qualification for the course was having 5 GCE's including Maths and English and I didn't possess these did I? The blow was devastating. No Lime Tree Place. No Electricity Board. No route to the top. Don Smith said there was just one hope though. He had influence with the college because the Board provided many candidates for courses and not least from the engineering side. He would put a case forward for getting exemption on the grounds of my experience to date coupled to the fact that the school I attended did not do GCE's. With a heavy heart I caught the bus back home. He was just being nice. There must be oodles of candidates with 5 GCE's. The date was 29th August 1960. Seven years later to the day, my first son would be born.

The letter came four days later. It bore a splendiferous letterhead, embossed and coloured and of a kind I had never seen before and from Lime Tree Place. I had got the job and when could I start and I was enrolled on the Business Administration Course starting in September. Whoopee for

Don Smith and whoopee for bell-ringing. I met John Smithson and bought him a pint.

It turned out that there were two financial benefits from my leaving British Railways at this time. Because my total service after the probationary period would be just under three years, I would in due course receive back my contributions from the Superannuation Scheme in full. The significance of this was apparent when six months later a cheque for £125 arrived. After sweating like a pig from having beaten the bus again on my battered cycle each morning and after work, the attraction of a certain shop window on Clumber Street begot a yearning satisfied by the purchase outright of a brand new and green Vespa 125 motor scooter. £97 plus road tax and insurance. The bill was exactly £125. Heaven sent. Years later in a lovely small private hotel in Amsterdam whilst cogitating on our backgrounds, I was to my surprise telling my boss that this act of purchase was the determining liberating factor in my life.

The second benefit was that the Provident Mutual contributions I had been making through the payroll each fortnight could be carried on after leaving the railway. The salesman who came around the office soon after I started had been persuasive but, because of my dire financial state, only to the tune of one shilling and six pence per week which was the very minimum contribution. Consequently, nineteen shillings and sixpence was forked out each quarter thereafter until it became £3 and eighteen shillings a year and later still a bit less when tax deduction at source came in. This policy premium was paid annually in sentimental memory of those first years in the Motive Power office and ran its full 30 year course. On leaving, Mr Jennings presented me with a Parker pen and propelling pencil set. The lads took me out for a drink and Lillian cried.

As it turned out, I was not going to be working at the romantically sounding Lime Tree Place after all. I was going to be this year's fast track management trainee spending six months in each of four departments, pre-billing, post-billing, credit control and possibly financial accounting - depending on my progress at college during the day release. Pre-billing was located in a satellite office above the electricity showrooms on Regent Street.

As was being discovered in the first few weeks and as would be reinforced more and more strongly with subsequent job moves, there are four discernable interactions taking place. At the highest level is the self-appraisal of whether the anticipated advantages over the previous job are actually there. The time saving and ease of getting from home to office were indeed major plus factors. The office was modern with proper desks and the work seemed to be fairly evenly distributed using laid down routines. The language and paperwork had a modern feel. A big tick there.

But what of number two, the disadvantages? The characters in the railway office left a big gaping hole. I was homesick for the bustle, the in-fighting, the scheming, the deadline pressure on timecards, the rows over Sunday rostering and most of all railway men from yardies to link 1 drivers in their issue uniforms dirty and clean bantering their way through a working week. And I missed the engines with their hissing, fizzing steam, their sheer size and power. And I missed the train journeys and travellers I had got to know so well. And I missed Nottingham with its traffic and shops and market and Herbert and the mini pork-pies.

At a third and fourth tangent are the surprise plus and surprise minus. One thing that never occurred in forethought was a different stature of work colleague arising. In this new office were young people, some younger than me. Most had good school leaving qualifications and all were well dressed and behaved. Not a single stand-up row or swear word in these early weeks. The ambience was businesslike and quiet. Was this what a modern office was really like? No ex-RAF officer or ex-army colonel or chief clerk from a Dickensian era with mature lady secretary flaunting herself in high-heels and overseen by a superintendent complete with bowler hat? Yes this surprise find was a plus. It felt a better place for me to be.

The surprise minus was the work type. Even after one week, that which was actually done appeared so mentally simple. Accuracy was obviously of the essence but comparisons with the wage calculations and mileage statistics of the last job left me both puzzled and worried. And so I sought for myself an honest conclusion. Had I made a good or bad decision?

I had wanted to get rid of the all-pervasive and debilitating tiredness, to cut down on wasted travelling time, to find a more modern industry and to seek a way to grow a career. But, deep down, there was a nagging feeling that I could have made a very bad mistake. If all that there was to this comfort was a routine checking future then I had to move quickly and push and push to get out and on.

Printed in Great Britain
by Amazon